THE
KAISER'S
CAPTIVE

IN THE CLAWS OF THE
GERMAN EAGLE

BY

ALBERT RHYS WILLIAMS

SPECIAL WAR CORRESPONDENT OF
THE OUTLOOK IN BELGIUM

Pen & Sword
MILITARY

This edition published in 2014 by

Pen & Sword Military
An imprint of
Pen & Sword Books Ltd
47 Church Street
Barnsley
South Yorkshire
S70 2AS

This book was first published as 'In the Claws of the German Eagle'
by E. P. Dutton & Co., New York, 1917.

Copyright © Coda Books Ltd.
Published under licence by Pen & Sword Books Ltd.

ISBN: 9781783463084

A CIP catalogue record for this book is available from the British Library

Printed and bound in England
By CPI Group (UK) Ltd, Croydon, CR0 4YY

Pen & Sword Books Ltd incorporates the imprints of Pen & Sword Aviation, Pen & Sword
Family History, Pen & Sword Maritime, Pen & Sword Military, Pen & Sword Discovery, Pen
& Sword Politics, Pen & Sword Atlas, Pen & Sword Archaeology, Wharncliffe Local History,
Wharncliffe True Crime, Wharncliffe Transport, Pen & Sword Select, Pen & Sword Military
Classics, Leo Cooper, The Praetorian Press, Claymore Press, Remember When, Seaforth
Publishing and Frontline Publishing

For a complete list of Pen & Sword titles please contact

PEN & SWORD BOOKS LIMITED
47 Church Street, Barnsley, South Yorkshire, S70 2AS, England
E-mail: enquiries@pen-and-sword.co.uk
Website: www.pen-and-sword.co.uk

TO THOSE WHO SEE
BEYOND THE RED
MISTS OF WAR

Acknowledgment

M Y THANKS GO to the Editors of *The Outlook* for permission to reproduce the articles which first appeared in that magazine.

Also to many friends all the way from Maverick to Pasadena. Above all to Frank Purchase, my comrade in the first weeks of the war and always.

CONTENTS

PART III
WITH THE WAR PHOTOGRAPHERS IN BELGIUM

PART IV
LOVE AMONG THE RUINS

INSTEAD OF A PREFACE

THE HORRIBLE AND incomprehensible hates and brutalities of the European War! Unspeakable atrocities! Men blood-lusting like a lot of tigers!

Horrible they are indeed. But my experiences in the war zone render them no longer incomprehensible. For, while over there, in my own blood I felt the same raging beasts. Over there, in my own soul I knew the shattering of my most cherished principles.

It is not an unique experience. Whoever has been drawn into the center of the conflict has found himself swept by passions of whose presence and power he had never dreamed.

For example: I was a pacifist bred in the bone. Yet, caught in Paris at the outbreak of the war, my convictions underwent a rapid crumbling before the rising tide of French national feeling. The American Legion exercised a growing fascination over me. A little longer, and I might have been marching out to the music of the *Marseillaise*, dedicated to the killing of the Germans. Two weeks later I fell under the spell of the self-same Germans. That long gray column swinging on through Liége so mesmerized me that my natural revulsion against slaughter was changed to actual admiration.

Had an officer right then thrust a musket into my hand, I could have mechanically fallen into step and fared forth to the killing of the French. Such an experience makes one chary about dispensing counsels of perfection to those fighting in the vortex of the world-storm. Whenever I begin to get shocked at the black crimes of the belligerents, my own collapse lies there to accuse me.

It is in the spirit of a non-partisan, then, that this chronicle of adventure in those crucial days of the early war is written. It is a welter of experiences and reactions which the future may use as another first-hand document in casting up its own conclusions. There is no careful calling out of just those episodes which support a particular theory, such as the total and complete depravity of the German race.

Despite my British ancestry, the record tries to be impartial - without pro- or anti-German squint. If the reader had been in my skin, zig-zagging his way through five different armies, the things which I saw are precisely the ones which he would have seen. So I am not to blame whether these episodes damn the Germans or bless them. Some do, and some don't. What one ran into was largely a matter of luck.

For example: In Brussels on September 27, 1914, I fell in with a lieutenant of the British army. With an American passport he had made his way into the city through the German lines. We both desired to see Louvain, but all passage thereto was for the moment forbidden. Starting out on the main road, however, sentry after sentry passed us along until we were halted near staff headquarters, a few miles out of the city, and taken before the commandant. We informed him of our overweening desire to view the ruins of Louvain. He explained, as sarcastically as he could, that war was not a social diversion, and bade us make a quick return to Brussels, swerving neither to the right nor left as we went.

As we were plodding wearily back, temptation suddenly loomed up on our right in the shape of a great gas-bag which we at first took to be a Zeppelin. It proved to be a stationary balloon which was acting as the eye of the artillery. It was signaling the range to the German gunners beneath, who were pounding away at the Belgians. In our excitement over the spectacle, we went plunging across fields until we gained a good view of the great swaying thing, tugging away at the slender filament of rope which bound it to the earth.

Sinking down into the grass, we were so intent upon the sharp electric signaling as to be oblivious to aught else, until a voice rang a harsh challenge from behind. Jumping to our feet, we faced a squad of German soldiers and an officer who said:

"What are you doing here?"

"Came out to see the big balloon," we somewhat naively informed him.

"Very good!" he said. And then, quite as if he were rewarding our manifest zeal for exploration, he added, "Come along with me and you can see the big commandant, too."

Three soldiers ahead and three behind, we were escorted down the railroad track in silence until we began to pass some cars filled with the recently wounded in a fearfully shot-to-pieces state. Some one mumbled "Englishmen!" and the whole crowd, bandaged and bleeding as they were, rose to the occasion and greeted us with derisive shouts.

"Put the blackguards to work," growled one.

"No! Kill the damn spies!" shouted another, as he pulled himself out of the straw, "kill them!"

A huge fellow almost wild from his wounds bellowed out: "Why don't you stick your bayonet into the cursed Englishmen!" No doubt it would have eased his pain a bit to see us getting a taste of the same thing he was suffering.

Our officer, as if to make concessions to this hue and cry, growled harshly: "Don't look around! Damn you! and take your hands out of your pockets!"

We heaved sighs of relief as we left this place of pain and hate behind. But a new terror took hold of us as a turn in the track brought our destination into view. It was the staff headquarters in which, two hours before, the commandant had ordered us to make direct return to Brussels.

"Wait here," said the officer as he walked inside.

We stood there trying to appear unconcerned while we cursed the exploring bent in our constitutions, and mentally composed farewell letters to the folks at home.

But luck does sometimes light upon the banners of the daring. It seems that in the two hours since we had left headquarters a complete change had been made in the staff. At any rate, an officer whom we had not seen before came out and addressed us in English. We told him that we were Americans.

"Well, let's see what you know about New York," he said.

We displayed au intensive knowledge of Coney Island and the Great White Way, which he deemed satisfactory.

"Nothing like them in Europe!" he assured us. "I did enjoy those ten years in America. I would do anything I could for one of you fellows."

He backed this up by straightway ordering our release, and authenticated his claim to American residence by his last shot:

"Now, boys, beat it back to Brussels."

We stood not on the order of our beating, but beat at once.

One may pick out of such an experience precisely what one wishes to pick out: the imbecile hatred in the Teuton - the perfidy of the British - the efficiency or the blundering of the German - or perchance the foolhardiness of the American, just as his nationalistic bias leads him.

So, from the narratives in this book, one may select just the material which supports his theory as to the merits or demerits of any nation. To myself, out of these insights into the Great Calamity, there has come reenforcement to my belief in the essential greatness of the human stuff in all nations. Along with this goes a faith that in the New Internationalism mankind will lay low the military Frankenstein that he has created, and realize the triumphant brotherhood of all human souls.

PART I
THE SPY-HUNTERS
OF BELGIUM

Chapter I
A Little German
Surprise Party

"TWO DAYS AND the French will be here! Three days at the outside, and not an ugly Boche left. Just mark my word!"

This the patriarchal gentleman in the Hôtel Métropole whispered to me about a month after the Germans had captured Brussels. They had taken away his responsibilities as President of the Belgian Bed Cross, so that now he had naught to do but to sit upon the lobby divan, of which he covered much, being of extensive girth. But no more extensive than his heart, from which radiated a genial glow of benevolence to all - all except the invaders, the sight or mention of whom put harshness in his face and anger in his voice.

"Scabbard-rattler!" he mumbled derisively, as an officer approached. "Clicks his spurs to get attention I Wants yon to look at him. Don't you do it. I never do." He closed his eyes tightly, as if in sleep.

Oftentimes he did not need to feign his slumber. But sinking slowly down into unconsciousness his native gentleness would return and a smile would rest upon his lips; I doubt not that in his dreams the Green-Gray troops of Despotism were ridden down by the Blue and Red Republicans of France.

Once even he hummed a snatch of the *Marseillaise*. An extra loud blast from the distant cannonading stirred him from his reverie.

"Ah ha!" he exclaimed, clasping my arm, "the artillery - it's getting nearer all the time. They are driving back the Bodies, eh? We'll be free to-morrow, certain. Then we'll celebrate together in my country-home."

Walking over to the door, he peered down the street as if he already expected to catch a glint of the vanguard of the Blue and Red. Twice he did this and returned with confidence unshaken.

"Mark my word," he reiterated; "three days at the outside and we shall see the French!"

That was in September, 1914. Those three days passed away into as many weeks, into as many months, and into almost as many years. I cannot help wondering whether the same hopes stirred within him at each fresh outburst of cannonading on the Somme. And whether through those soul-sickening months that white-haired man peered daily down those Brussels streets, yearning for the advent of the Red and Blue Army of Deliverance. Red and Blue it was ever in his mind. If once it had come in its new uniform of somber hue, it would have been a disappointing shock I fear. He was an old man then; he is now perhaps beyond all such human hurts. His pain was as real as anything I saw in all the war. I had little time to dwell upon it, however, for presently I was put into a situation that called for all my wits. I was introduced to it by the announcement of the porter:

"An American gentleman to see you, sir."

That was joyful news to one held within the confines of a captive city, from which all exit was, for the time being, closely barred.

It was September 28th, my birthday, too. The necessity of celebrating this in utter boredom was a dismal prospect. Now this came upon me like a little surprise-party.

Picking up a bit of paper on which I had been scribbling down a few memoranda that I feared might escape my mind, I hastened into the hallway to meet a somewhat spare, tall, and extremely erect-appearing man. He greeted me with a smile and a bow - a rather dry smile and a rather stiff bow for an American.

So I queried, "You're an American, are you?"

"Not exactly," he responded; "but I would like to talk with you."

Without the shadow of a suspicion, I told him it would be a great relief from the tedium of the day to talk to any one.

"But I would prefer to talk to you in your room," he added.

"Certainly," I responded, stepping toward the elevator.

The hotel was practically deserted, so I was somewhat surprised when two men, one a huge fellow built on a superdreadnaught plan, followed us in and got out with us on the fifth floor. The superdreadnaught sailed on into my room, which seemed a breach of propriety for an unintroduced stranger. He closed the door rudely behind him. I was prepared to resent this altogether high-handed intrusion, when my tall guest said, very simply, "I am representing the Imperial German Government."

I rallied under the shock sufficiently to say, "Will you take a chair?"

"No," came the laconic reply, "I will take you - and this," he said, reaching for the piece of scribble-paper I had in my hands, "and any baggage you have in your room."

I assured him that I had none, as I really expected to stay in Brussels but a day. He pretended not to hear my reply, and said,

"We better take it with us, for we will probably need it."

He looked under the bed and unlocked the closet door. Finding nothing, he asked for the key to my room. I handed it over, Boom Number 502.

"You will be so good as to follow me now."

Now every one knows that the Spy-Season in Europe opened with the beginning of the war. Spy hunting became at once a veritable mania.

Consequently no self-respecting person returns from the war-zone without at least one hair-raising story of being taken as a spy. Being just an average species of American, I exhale no particular air of mystery or villainy; yet I suffered a score of times the laying on of hands by German, French, Belgian, and even Dutch authorities.

But this experience is marked off from all my other ordeals in four ways. In the first place, instead of casually falling into the hands of my captors, they came after me in full force. In the second place, a specific charge of using money for bribing information was laid against me, and witnesses were at hand. In the third place, the leader of the party arrested me in civilian dress, but before examination and trial he changed to military uniform. In the fourth place, the officials were in such a surly mood that my message to the American Ambassador was undelivered, and at the last trial before the American representatives there was no apology, but rather the sullen attitude of those who had been balked in bagging their game.

When my captor bade me follow him I asked:

"Can I leave word with my friends?" For an answer he smiled satirically. By accident or design, the time chosen for my taking off was one when both of my two casual acquaintances were out of the hotel.

"Not now, but a little later perhaps, when this is fixed up," my captor answered me.

We stepped into a carriage. The two assistants at the little surprise party walked away, and my rising sense of fear was allayed by the friendly offer of a cigarette. It was a brand-new experience to ride away to prison in royal state like this. The almost pleasant attitude of my companion reassured me. "After all," I mused, "this is a lucky stroke; a little uncertain perhaps, but on the whole an interesting way to while away the tedium of an otherwise eventless birthday."

We stopped before the Belgian Government building, on the *Rue de la Loi*, the headquarters of the German staff. At a word the sentries dropped back and my companion bade me walk down a long, dark corridor. I opened a door at the end, and found myself in a room with a few officers in chairs, and a large array of documents upon a table.

The moment I came within the safe confines of that room the whole attitude of my captor changed. His mask of friendliness dropped away. Perhaps his spirit responded and adapted itself to the official atmosphere of the headquarters. Anyhow, at once he froze up into the most rigid formality. Sitting down, he wrote out what I deemed was the report of the morning's proceedings. I watched him writing with all the semblance and precision of a machine, except for a half-smile that sometimes flickered upon his close-pressed lips.

He was a machine, or, more precisely, a cog in the great fighting machine that was producing death and destruction to Belgium. Just as the Germans have put men through a certain mold and turned out the typical German soldier, in like manner through other molds they have turned out according to pattern the German secret service man. He is a kind of spy-destroyer performing in his sphere the same service that the torpedo-boat destroyer does in its domain. This man was the German reincarnation of Javert, the police inspector who hung so relentlessly upon the flanks of Jean Valjean. In his stolid silence I read an iron determination to "get" me, and in that flickering smile I saw an inhuman delight in putting the worst construction upon my case as he wrote it down. Hereafter he shall be known as Javert.

Towards Javert I sustain a very distinct aversion. This is not the result of any evil twist put into my constitution by original sin. Quite the contrary. Hitherto I have always felt that I, like the man in Oscar Wilde's play, could forgive anybody anything, any time, anywhere. One can forgive even a hangman for doing his duty, however it may thwart one's plans. Some men must play the part of prosecutor and devil's advocate.

But such was the cold, cynical delight in this fellow's doing his duty, such was his arrogant, overbearing attitude toward the helpless peasant prisoners, that I know my prayers for the end of the war were not motived entirely by selfless considerations. I am hankering to get into the neighborhood of this fellow when he doesn't hold all the trump cards. In justice to Javert, I must say that he reciprocated my feeling magnificently, and, inasmuch as he was the cat and I the mouse, and a very small one at that, he probably found much more spiritual satisfaction in the exercise of his feelings than I did in mine. That is why I was anxious to have the war end and embrace the first opportunity to change our roles. I yearned to give him his proper place in the sun.

Having completed my case, he demanded my papers, and then bade me open the door. There was a soldier waiting, and with him ahead and Javert behind, I was escorted into the courtyard. Here a double-door was opened, and I was thrust into a room filled with a motley collection of persons guarded by a dozen soldiers with rifles ready.

The sight was anything but reassuring. I turned toward Javert and asked, somewhat frantically, I fear: "What is all this for? Aren't you going to do anything about my case?"

My hitherto cool, smiling manner must have been an irritation to him. A German official, especially a petty one, takes everything with such deadly seriousness that he can't understand us taking things so debonairly, especially when it is his own magisterial self.

So I think he thoroughly enjoyed my first signs of perturbation, and said: "Your case will be settled in a little while - perhaps directly." He turned to a soldier, bade him watch me, and disappeared.

About five minutes later I heard outside the command "Halt!" to a squad of soldiers. The doors opened and Javert reappeared, this time in the full uniform of an officer. For the moment I thought he had come with a firing squad and they were going to make short shrift of me. The grim humor of disposing of my case thus "directly" came home to me. But merely flicking the ashes from his cigarette, he glanced round the room without offering the slightest recognition, and then disappeared. How he made his change from civilian clothes so quickly I can't understand. It seemed like a vainglorious display of his uniform in order to let us take full cognizance of his eminence.

I began now a survey of my surroundings. Our room was in fact a hallway crammed with soldiers and prisoners. The soldiers, with fixed bayonets in their rifles, stood guard at the door. The prisoners, some thirty-five in number, were ranged on benches, overturned boxes, and on the floor. We were of every description, from well-groomed men of the city to artisans and peasants from the fields. The most interesting of the peasants was a young fellow charged with carrying dispatches through the lines to Antwerp. The most interesting of the well-dressed urban group was a theater manager charged with making his playhouse the center of distribution for the forbidden newspapers smuggled into Brussels. There was a Belgian soldier in uniform, woefully battered and beaten; and for the first time I saw a German soldier without his rifle. He, too, was a prisoner waiting trial, having been sent up to the headquarters accused of muttering against an under officer.

All these facts I learned later. Then I sat paralyzed in an atmosphere charged with smoke and silence. The smoke came not from the prisoners, for to them it was forbidden, but from the soldiers, who rolled it up in great clouds. The silence came from the suspicion that one's next neighbor might be a spy planted there to catch him in some unwary statement. Each man would have sought relief from the strain by unbosoming his hopes and fears to his neighbor, but he dared not. That is one fearful curse of any cause that is buttressed by a system of espionage. It scatters everywhere the seeds of suspicion. All society is shot through with cynical distrust. It poisons the springs at the very source - one's faith in his fellows. Ordinarily one regards the next man as a neighbor until he proves himself a spy. In Europe he is a scoundrel and a spy until he proves beyond the shadow of a doubt that he is a neighbor.

And then one is never certain. People were everywhere aghast to find even their life-long friends in the pay of the enemy, A large military establishment draws spies as certainly as a carcass draws vermin; the one is the inevitable concomitant of the other. It is the Nemesis of all human brotherhood.

Now to be taken as a prisoner of war was to most men more of a Godsend than a tragedy. The prisoner knew that he was to be corralled in a camp. But he was alive at any rate and he had but to await the end of the war - then it was home again. The pictures show phalanxes of these men smiling as if they were glad to be captives. On the other hand there are no smiles in the pictures of the spies and *francstireurs*. They know that they are fated for a hasty trial, a drumhead decision, and to be shot at dawn. The prospect of that walk through the early morning dews to the execution-ground made their shoulders droop along with their spirits.

With these thoughts on our mind we held our tongues and kept our eyes on the door, wondering who would be the next guest to arrive, and mentally conjecturing what might be the cause of his incarceration.

The last arrival wore a small American flag wound round his arm, and around his waist he wore a belt which contained 100 pounds in gold. He spotted me, and, coming over to my corner, opened up a conversation in English. I thought at first that this was merely a clumsy German ruse to trap me into some indiscreet talking. To his kindly advances I curtly returned "Yeses" and "Noes."

His name was Obels, a Belgian by birth but speaking English as well as German, French, and Flemish. He was an invaluable reporter for a great Chicago paper, and in his zeal for news had run smack into the Germans at Malines, and had been at once whisked off by automobile to Brussels for trial as a spy. He had a passionate devotion to his calling. No mystic could have been more consecrated to his Holy Church. I fully believe that he would have consented to be shot as a spy with a smile on his face if he could have got the story of the shooting to his paper. He was one of the most straightforth fellows I have ever met, and yet I regarded him there as I would a low-browed scoundrel. For a long time I would not speak to him. I dared not. He might have been a spy set to worm out any confidences, and then carry them to Javert.

Left to himself, each man let his most pessimistic thoughts drag his spirits down. Gloom is contagious, and it soon became as heavy in the room as the gray clouds of smoke. The one bright, hopeful spot was the lone woman prisoner. She alone refused to succumb to the depressing atmosphere, and sought to play woman's ancient role of comforter. She tried to smile, and succeeded admirably, for she was very pretty. A wretched-looking lad huddled up on a bag in the comer tried to reciprocate, but with the tears glistening in his eyes he made a sorry failure of it. We were a hard crowd to smile to, and growing tired of her attempts to appear light-hearted, she at last gave herself up to her own grievances, and soon was looking quite as doleful as the rest of us. Our gloom was thrown into sharp relief by a number of soldiers grouped around a table in the corner laughing and shouting over a game of cards which they were playing for small stakes. We dragged out the long afternoon staring doggedly at the bayonets of our guards.

Only once did the guards show any awareness of our existence. That was when suddenly the arrival of "Herr Major" was announced. As the door was opened to let him pass through our hall to the stairway, with a hoarse shout we were ordered to our feet. As his exalted personage paraded by we stood, hats in hand, with bared heads, with such humble and respectful expression as may be outwardly assumed towards a fellow-being whom all secretly despised or desired to kill. Was there really a murderous gleam in the averted eyes of those Belgians arrayed in salute before the Herr Major, or was it my imagination that put it there? Perhaps you can tell.

Picture your country devastated, your towns burned, your flag prohibited, your farmers shot, your women and children terrified, your papers and public meetings suppressed, your streets patrolled by aliens with drawn swords as your enemies' bands triumphantly play their national airs. Picture, then, yourself lied about by hireling spies, thrown into prison, compelled to breathe foul air and sleep upon a floor, fed on black bread, and held day after day for sentence in nerve-racking suspense. Picture to yourself now the abject humiliation of being compelled to stand bare-headed in salute before these wreckers and spoilers of your land. Do you think you might keep back from your eyes sparks from that blazing rebellion in your soul? Then it was not imagination that made me see the murderous gleam in the eyes of those high-spirited Belgians. "Salute the Major!" the Germans shouted. What seeds of hate those words planted in those Belgian souls the future will show, when they who sow the wind shall reap the whirlwind.

That is the unseen horror of war; pictures can reveal the damage wrought by shot and shell, fire and flood in the blasted cities and in the fields of the dead. Bat nothing can ever show the irreparable spiritual damage wrought to the human soul by hates, humiliations, fears and undying animosities.

CHAPTER II
SWEATING UNDER THE GERMAN THIRD DEGREE

B Y THIS TIME my lark-like spirit of the morning had folded its wings. My musings took on a decidedly somber tinge. "Were the Germans going to make a summary example of me to warn outsiders to cease prowling around the war zone?" "Was I going to be railroaded off to jail, or even worse?" It was no time to be wool gathering! It was high time for doing. "But what pretexts could they find for such action?" At any rate I resolved to furnish as few pretexts as possible.

I set to work hunting carefully through my pockets for everything that might furnish the slightest basis for any charge against me. Before coming to Brussels I had been warned not to carry anything that might be the least incriminating, and there was not much on me; but I did have a pass from the Belgian commander giving me access to the Antwerp fortifications. I had figured on framing it as a souvenir of my adventures, but my molars now reduced it to an unrecognizable pulp. Cards of introduction from French and English friends fared a similar fate. Their remains were disposed of in the shuffling that accompanied the arrival of new prisoners. This had to be done most craftily, for we never knew where were the spying eyes.

About six o'clock I was resting from my masticatory labors when Javert presented himself, accompanied by two soldiers. I was led away into the council room where first I had been taken in the morning. It was now turned into a trial chamber. Javert, as prosecutor, was seated on one side of the table, while around the farther end were ranged some officers and a few men in civilian clothes who proved to be secret service agents. I stood until the judge bade me take my seat at the vacant end of the table.

One by one my documents were disposed of - an American passport issued in London; a permit from the German Consul at Maastricht, Holland, to enter "the territory of Belgium-Germany," finally, this letter of introduction from the American Consulate at Ghent:

Consulat Americain.
Gand le 22 Septembre, 1914.
Le Consul des Etats Unis d'Amerique a Gand, prie Messieurs les autorites de bien vouloir laisser passer le porteur de la presente Monsieur Albert Williams citoyen Americain.
JULIUS VAN HEE,
Consul Americain.

I pointed to the recent date on it, the 22nd of September, and to the signer of it, Julius van Hee.

Van Hee was a man who met the Germans on their own ground. He informed the German officer at his hotel: "If you send any spy prowling into my room, I'll take off my coat and proceed to throw him out of the window." Shirt-sleeves diplomat indeed! Another time he requested permission to take three Belgian women through the lines to their family in Bruges. The German commandant said "No." "All right," said Van Hee, taking out a package of letters from captured German officers who were now in the hands of the Belgians, and dangling the packet before the commandant, "If I don't get that permit, you don't get these letters." He got the permit.

After a few such clashes the invaders learned that when it came to this *Schrecklichkeit* business they had no monopoly on the article. Van Hee's name was not to be trifled with. But on the other hand there must necessarily have existed a certain resentment against him for his ruthless and effective diplomacy. It would no doubt afford Javert a pleasant sensation to take it out on any one appearing in any way as a protégé of Van Hee.

"Yes, it's Van Hee's signature all right," muttered Javert with a shrug of his shoulders, "only he is not the consul, but the vice-consul at Ghent and let us remember that he is of Belgian ancestry - that wouldn't incline him to deep friendship with us."

On a card of introduction from Ambassador Van Dyke there were the words "Writer for *The Outlook*." It's hard to understand how that escaped my very scrutinous search, but there it was.

"Another anti-German magazine," Javert commented, sardonically. I was marveling at the uncanny display of knowledge of this man at the center of the European maelstrom, aware of the editorial policy of an American magazine.

"But that doesn't mean that I am anti-German," I protested; "we can retain our own private opinions."

"Tommyrot," exclaimed Javert, "tommyrot!" Strange language in a military court! Where had he laid hold of that choice bit of our vernacular?

"You know perchance," he continued, "what the penalty is for newspaper men caught on the German side." I thought that surely I was going to reap the result of the adverse reports that the American correspondents had made already about the Germans, when he added, "But you are here on a different charge."

The judge started to cross-examine me as to all my antecedents. My replies were in German - or purported to be - but in my eagerness to clear myself I must have wrought awful havoc with that classic language. I was forthwith ordered to talk English and direct my remarks to Javert, acting now as interpreter. In the midst of this procedure Javert, with a quick sudden stroke, produced the scribble-paper which he had seized in the morning, held it fairly in my face, and cried, "Whose writing is that?" The others all riveted their gaze upon me.

I replied calmly, "It is mine."

"I want you to put it into full, complete writing," cried Javert. "As it now stands it is a telegraphic code."

That is the most complimentary remark that has ever been made upon my hieroglyphics. However, I shall be eternally grateful to

Providence for my Horace Greeley style. For, while that document contained by no means any military secrets, there were, on the other hand, uncomplimentary observations about the Germans. It would not be good strategy to let these fall into their hands in their present mood. At Javert's behest, I set to work on my paper, and delivered to him in ten minutes a free, full, rapid translation of the abbreviated contents. On inspecting it Javert said, irritably, "I want an exact, precise transcript of everything here."

"I thought you wanted it in a hurry," I rejoined.

"No hurry at all. We have ample time to fix your case."

These words do not sound a bit threatening, but it was the general setting in which they were said that made them so ominous, and which set the cold waves rippling up and down my spinal column.

I set to work again, numbering every phrase in my scribble-paper, and then in the same number on the other paper giving a full, readable translation of it. I wrote out the things complimentary to the Germans in the fullest manner. But how was I going to take the sting out of the adverse comments?

Phrase No. 1 meant "Musical nature of the German automobile horns." Their silver and flute-like notes had been a pleasing sound, rolling along the roads. That was good.

Phrase No, 2 meant "The moderation of the Germans in not billeting more troops upon the hotels." I wondered why they had not commandeered quarters in more of the big empty hotels instead of compelling men to sleep in railway stations and in the open air. That was good.

Phrase No. 3 meant "German officers never refused to contribute to the Belgian Relief Funds." These boxes were constantly shaken before them in every café, and not once was a box passed to an officer in vain. For all this I was very grateful and everything went on very merrily until I came to phrase Number 4.

"If Bel I wld join posse Ger myself"; which, being interpreted, reads, "If I were a Belgian, I would join a posse against the Germans myself." That looked ugly, but I wanted to record for myself the ugly mood of resentment I had felt when I saw Belgians compelled to submit to certain humiliations and indignities from their invading conquerors.

German or non-German - it makes no difference; any one who had seen those swaggering officers riding it rough-shod over those poor peasants, would have felt the same tide of indignation mounting up in him. In that mood it would have given me genuine pleasure to have joined a little killing-party and wiped out those officers. Now these self-same officers were gathered round me trying to decide whether they were to have a little killing-party on their own account.

There was sufficient justification for inciting their wrath in that one sentence as it stood, and they were all combining to entrap me by every possible means. Furthermore, they were hankering for a victim. I had only my wits to match against their desires. I cudgeled my brains as I never did before, but to no avail. Almost panic-stricken I was ready to give up in despair and throw myself upon the mercy of the court when, like a flash of inspiration, the right reading came. I transcribed that ugly phrase now to read: "If I were among the Belgians, I would join possibly the Germans myself." What more could the most ardent German patriot ask for? That met every abbreviation and made a beautifully exact reversal of the intended meaning. Not as an example in ethics, but as a "safety first" exhibit I must confess to a real pride in that piece of work. I handed it over with the cherubic expression of the prize-scholar in the Sunday School.

Javert had figured on finding incriminating data in it. It was to be his chief evidence. He read it over with increasing disappointment and gave it the minutest analysis, comparing it closely with the original scribble-paper. For example, he called the attention of the judge to the fact that "guarded" in one paper was spelled "gaurded" in the other - some slip I had inadvertently made. He thought it might now be made a clew to some secret code, but, though he puzzled long and searchingly over the document, he extracted from it nothing more than an increased vexation of spirit.

"Nothing on the surface here," Javert said to the judge; "but that only makes it look the more suspicious. Wait till we hear from the search of his room."

At this juncture a man in civilian dress arrived, and, handing over the key of Room Number 502, reported that there was nothing to bring back. This nettled Javert, and he made and X-ray examination of my person, even tearing out the lining of my hat. Alas for him! too late; his search disclosed nothing more damnatory than a French dictionary, which, because I was not an ostrich, I had been unable to get away with in the afternoon. A few addresses had been scribbled therein. He demanded a full account of each name. Some I had really forgotten.

"That's strange," he sneered; "perhaps you don't find it convenient to remember who they are."

Up till now I hadn't the slightest conception of the charge laid against me. Suddenly the judge crashed into the affair and took the initiative.

"Why did you offer money to find out the movement of German troops?" he let go at me across the table in a loud voice.

At the same time his aides converged on me a full, searching gaze. Going all day without food, for eight hours confined in a fetid atmosphere, and for two hours grilled by a dozen inquisitors, is an ordeal calculated to put the nerves of the strongest on edge.

I simply replied, "I didn't do any such thing."

"Don't lie!" "Tell the whole truth!" "Make a clean breast of it!" "No use holding anything back!" "We have the witnesses who will swear you did!" "Best thing for you is to tell all you know!"

This fusillade of command and accusation they roared and bellowed at me, aiming to break down my defense with the suddenness of the onslaught. They succeeded for a moment. I couldn't rally my scattered and worn-out wits to think what the basis of this preposterous charge might be.

Then I remembered a Dutchman who had accosted me the day before on a street-car. He had volunteered the information that he was taking people by automobile out through Liége into Holland, giving one thus the opportunity to see a great many troops and ruins along the way. I told him I had some money and would be glad to invest in such a trip, at the same time giving him my address at the Hôtel Métropole. Guileless as he appeared, he turned out to be an agent of the German Government. He naturally wanted to make himself solid with his masters by delivering the goods, so he had twisted all my words into the most damning evidence, and had fixed up two or three witnesses ready to swear anything.

"No use wasting time or effort to save this man," they told de Leval at the American Embassy, later. "We've got a cast-iron case against him, with witnesses to back it up."

Javert no doubt proved himself an invaluable ally of the Dutchman in fixing up the charges. I don't believe he would manufacture a story out of whole cloth, but once his mind was set in a certain direction he could build up a good one on very shaky foundations. Perhaps he had an animus against these bumptious, undeferential, overcritical Americans, and thought it was time to give one of them a lesson. Perhaps he was tired of trapping ordinary garden variety spies of the Belgian brand. It would be a pleasing variation in the monotony of convicting defenseless, helpless Belgians if he could show that one of these fellows masquerading as Americans was a sham. Especially one of that journalistic tribe that had been sending out reports of German atrocities. Furthermore, it would redound greatly to his professional glory to hand me over to the General with a case proved to the hilt.

There was no trick in the repertory of a prosecutor that was unknown to Javert. He now shifted to the confidential and dropping his voice very low, he said to me:

"You know that if you make a full, complete confession, I'll promise to do my very best for you. And as a matter of fact you have been under the eyes of our Secret Service ever since you came to Belgium. We are aware of everything that you have done."

Was that a bluff or the truth? If it was true then they knew about my capture near Louvain on the day before in suspicious observation of the signaling-balloon. If this was a bluff, then my confession would be simply a case of gratuitously damning myself and likewise endangering my companion of yesterday's adventure - the British lieutenant with the

American passport. Yet again if Javert knew all he pretended to, silence about that episode would make it appear doubly heinous. So while with my tongue I retailed a simple, harmless version of my doings in Belgium in my brain I carried on a debate whether to make an avowal of the Louvain escapade or not.

I came to the decision that Javert was just bluffing. Later developments proved me right. He knew nothing about it Even the German Secret Service is not omniscient. Getting no results then from these wheedling tactics Javert shifted back to his bullying and essayed once more to browbeat me into a confession. Calling to his aid two officers who had been but casual onlookers they began volleying charges at me with machine-gun rapidity.

"You know that you are a spy." "We know that you are a spy." "Why do you deny it?" "You know that you have been lying." "Better own up to all that you have done." "Out with it now!"

When one officer grew tired, he rested. Then the next one took up the attack, and then he rested. But not one moment's respite for me. I don't know what they call it in German, but it was the third degree with a vengeance. Under this sweating process my nerves were being torn to tatters. I felt like screaming and it seemed that if this continued I would smash an officer with a chair and put an end to it all. But the fact that I am writing these lines shows that I didn't. Human nature is so constituted that it can always endure a little more, and though they kept the tension high for many minutes I did not buckle under the strain. However, I couldn't call up any arguments to show the utter absurdity of the charge against me. And my defense was very feeble.

The onslaught now ceased as suddenly as it had begun. There was a coming and going of officers and some consultation in an undertone. The judge left the room and the impassive-faced Javert began that machine-like writing. After a while he stopped.

"Will you give me some idea of what you expect to do with me?" I queried.

"A full report of your case goes up to the General for decision and sentence," was his response.

My spirits took a downward plunge. Then a fierce resentment amounting almost to rage came surging up within me. Masking it as well as I could, I asked permission to send word to the American authorities. Javert's reply was evasive.

"I have had nothing to eat all day," I announced. "Can't you do something for me?"

"Go to that door there and open it," said Javert.

I did so and there stood four soldiers of the Kaiser, who ranged themselves two in front and two behind, and marched me away. Javert had a well-developed sense of the dramatic.

While I am excoriating Javert as representing the genius of German officialdom, it is only fair that I should present his antithesis. By continually referring to the German army as a machine one gets the idea that it is an impersonal collection of inhuman beings remorselessly and mechanically devoted to duty. For a broad general impression that is perhaps a fair enough statement to start with; but when I am tempted to let it go at that, there is one striking exception that always rises up to point the finger of denial at this easy and common generalization.

It is that of a young German officer, a mere stripling of twenty or thereabouts, with the most frank, open, ingenuous expression. One would expect to find him presiding at a Christian Endeavor social, rather than right here at the very pivot of the most terrible military organization of the world.

I had caught his look riveted upon me in my trial, and recognized him when he came into the detention-room, to which the four soldiers had led me. Hurriedly, he said to me: "Really, you know, I ought not to come in here, but I heard your story, and it looks rather bad; but somehow I almost believe in you. Tell me the whole truth about your affair."

I proceeded vehemently to point out my innocence, when he interrupted my story by asking, "But why did you make that *Schreibfehler* on your paper?" He followed my recital anxiously and sympathetically, and, looking me full in the face, asked, "Can you tell me on your *Ehrenwort* (word of honor) that you are not a spy? Remember," he added, solemnly, "on your *Ehrenwort*."

Grasping both of his hands and looking him in the eye, I said, most fervently, "On my *Ehrenwort*, I am not a, spy."

There was an earnestness in my heart that must have communicated itself to "my hands, because he winced as he drew his hands away; but he said, I shall try to put in a word for you; I can't do much, but I shall do what I can. I must go now. Good-by."

CHAPTER III
A NIGHT ON A
PRISON FLOOR

"**P**RISONERS ARE TO be taken over into the left wing for the night," said an orderly to the guards.

We had scarcely turned the comer, when an officer cried: "Not that way, *dummkopf!*"

"Our orders are for the left wing, sir," said the orderly.

"Never saw such a set of damned blockheads!" yelled the officer in exasperation. "Can't you tell the difference between right and left? Right wing, right wing, and hurry up!"

A little emery had gotten into the perfect-running machine. The corridors fairly clanged with orders and counter orders. After much confusion the general mix-up of prisoners was straightened out and we were served black bread and coffee.

The strain of the day, along with the fever I had from exposure on the battlefields, made the rough food still more uninviting, especially as our only implements of attack were the greasy pocketknives of the peasants and canteen covers from the soldiers. The revolt of my stomach must have communicated itself to my soul. I determined for aggressive action on my own behalf. I resolved to stand unprotesting no longer while a solid case against me was being constructed. Not without a struggle was I to be railroaded off to prison or to Purgatory. Pushing up to the next officer appearing in the room, in firm but courteous tones I requested, as an American citizen, the right to communicate with the American authorities.

He replied very decently that that was quite within my privileges, and forthwith the opportunity would be accorded me. I was looking for paper, when there came the order for all of us to move out into the courtyard. With a line of soldiers on either side, we were marched through labyrinthine passages and up three flights of stairs. Here we were divided into two gangs, my gang being led off into a room already nearly filled. We were told that it was our temporary abode, and we were to make the best of it. It was an administrative office of the Belgian Government now turned into a prison. There were the usual fixtures, including a rug on the floor and shelves of books. Ours was only one of many cells for prisoners scattered through the building. The spy-hunters had swooped down upon every suspect in Belgium and all who had been caught in the dragnet were being dumped into these rooms.

We were thus informed by the officer whose wards we were. He was a fussy, quick-tempered, withal kind-hearted little fellow, and kept dashing in and out of the room, really perplexed over housing accommodations for the night. The spy-hunters had been successful in their work of rounding up their victims from all over the country and corralling them here until the place was filled to overflowing. Our official in charge was puffed up with pride in the prosperity of his institution, on the one hand, and, on the other hand, petulantly belectured us on adding ourselves to his already numerous burdens. This was highly humorous, yet we all feared to commit *lèse-majesté* by expressing to him our collective and personal sorrow for so inconveniencing him, and our willingness to make amends for our thoughtlessness in getting arrested.

After more hesitation than I had hitherto observed, arrangements for the night were completed and we were ordered to draw out blankets from the pile in the corner. The new arrivals and the old inmates maneuvered for the softest spots on the floor, which was soon covered over with bodies and their sprawling limbs, while a host of guards, fully armed, were posted at the door and along the hall.

"I would give my right arm or my leg if I could get a flashlight of this," said Obels, the reporter, enthusiastically. This elation made him reckless as he went about, probing the experiences of each victim.

"Great stuff!" "Great stuff!" he kept exclaiming. "Won't this open up some eyes in Chicago, eh?"

He couldn't believe that the Providence which had led him to this

Bonanza would now deny him the opportunity of getting out some of this wealth.

In the midst of these activities he was haled before the tribunal. He returned, the spring out of his step and his zest for stories quite gone. Javert had successively branded him an "Idiot" a "Liar" and a "Spy."

The information that several of the inmates had been imprisoned for a month or more spurred my drooping spirits and put me into action. I uncovered a pile of the office writing-paper and, with the aid of the Belgian who could speak English, I set to work preparing a letter to Ambassador Whitlock. Whether Javert was apprised of the doings of his charges or not I do not know, but in the midst of my writing he glided into the room, and, pouncing upon my manuscript, gathered it to himself, saying, "I'll take these." My Belgian friend protested that a superior officer had given me permission to do this. Javert handed back the paper, smiled, and disappeared. Knowing that every word would be closely scrutinized at the Staff Office, and that the least hint of anything derogatory to the German authorities would keep the letter in the building, I couched it in as pointed and telling terms as possible, having in mind the eyes of the Germans, quite as much as the Ambassador.

Brand Whitlock,
United States Ambassador, Brussels.

DEAR SIR:

As a native American citizen, born in Ohio, and now imprisoned by the German authorities, I claim your intervention in my behalf. I am thirty years of age, resident of East Boston, Massachusetts, for six years. I am a graduate of Marietta College, Hartford Seminary, and studied in Cambridge University in England, and Marburg University in Germany.

Saturday Mr. Van Hee, the American consul at Ghent, brought me here by automobile with Mr. Fletcher. Obliged to take back in his car three ladies for whom he obtained permission from the German Government, I was necessarily left behind; Mr. Van Hee promising to return for me when diplomatic business brought him to Brussels in a few days. Meantime I took a room at the Hôtel Métropole. From it I was taken by the German authorities this morning. I do not know exactly what the charge against me is. I am accused of offering money for information relative to the movement of the German troops. I think that the man who worked up the case against me is a Dutchman with whom I spoke upon a car. He volunteered the information that he had been everywhere by automobile; and I asked him if he was the one who carried passengers out of Brussels by way of Liége and Aix-la-Chapelle. Won't you look into my case at once? Mr. Fletcher, who called on you Saturday, lent me some fifty dollars, so I am all right that way; but this is not a comfortable situation to be in, though the officers are very decent. If you want proof of my identity, you can communicate with the following people in America; they are my personal friends, and will confirm my absence from home on an extended vacation.

His Excellency Governor Walsh, of the Commonwealth of Massachusetts; Dr. Charles Fleischer, Chief Rabbi in the Rabbinate of New England.

(If there was any Jewish blood on the German Staff I was going to try to get the benefit of it.)

The Honorable George W. Coleman, of the Ford Hall Convocatiott Meetings and President of the Pilgrim Amalgamated Associated Advertising Clubs of America.

(Coleman being a cross between a Baptist deacon and an anarchist, I knew that he would not object to this bit of sabotage.)

The Right Honorable William W. Mills, Esquire, President of the First National Bank of Marietta, Ohio, Treasurer of the University of Marietta, and Member of the National Council of Congregational Churches of America, etc., etc.

If you will cablegram any of these, you will get an immediate reply.
While I have no money for this now, I feel certain Mr. Fletcher, who
is associated with Mr. Lane, of the United States Cabinet, will back
you up, and there will be unlimited funds in America.

Sincerely yours,
ALBERT R. WILLIAMS.

My attention has been called to the omission of the Angel Gabriel, Mary Pickford and Ty Cobb from the list of my intimate friends in the above document. That was not meant as a slight - purely an oversight. At any rate, I felt that the long list of men whose names were written here would make the right response to any cablegram. To atone for dragging them into the affray I call attention to the highly deferential and decorative manner in which I referred to them. Be it remembered that this document was prepared quite as much for German eyes as for the Ambassador's, and nothing gives a man standing and respect in the Teutonic mind as much as a name fearfully and wonderfully adorned. I resolved that my importance was not to suffer from lack of glory in my friends. I bestowed more honorary degrees on them than the average small college does in ten commencements. So lavish was I that my friends hardly recognize their own titular selves.

An officer designated the guard who would deliver the letter. I gave it to him along with a franc, which he protestingly accepted. He reported that it was delivered to Javert. That was the last I ever heard from that message. I imagine that it was by no means the last that the German authorities heard from it, for when I related the story to the Ambassador some time later I saw a characteristic Brand Whitlock letter a-brewing. My message to Vice-Consul Naesmith and to the Hôtel Métropole shared a like fate - they were undelivered.

I simply offer the facts as they are. It may be that the courtesies of polite intercourse are not easy to observe in war. Certainly they were not obtrusive in Belgium. In extenuation it may be said that the Brussels postmen had struck about this time; but, on the other hand, through the forbidden shutters I saw fully fifty German Boy Scouts marshaled in the courtyard below.

I had noticed them before as messengers going down the most unguarded by-ways of the slums, quite as if they were agents of a welcomed instead of hated army. They rode along serenely as if totally unconscious of the shining targets that they made. I felt certain that no American gang would let slip this opportunity for the heaving of a brick. Were Brussels boys made of flabbier stuff! Not if Belgian sons were of the same stripe as Belgian fathers. The fact then that none of these German Scouts were massacred, as was to be expected by all the rules of the game, showed how the threat of reprisals operated to curb the strongest natural impulses of the spirit. I presumed that one of these Scouts was speeding post-haste to the Ambassador with my note, but he never did.

I am not berating the Germans. They were running their own war according to their own code. In this code reporters, onlookers, and uplifters of any brand were anathema.

We had no rights. Our only right was to the convictions within our minds, provided we kept them there. I believe that were it not for the surmises of the English lieutenant who took them to the Ambassador I would be in prison yet. On second thought, I wouldn't, either. I couldn't have endured the strain much longer. If I had been caged in there a few hours more than I was, in my nervous tension I probably would have vented my sense of outraged justice by assaulting one of the officers myself. I wouldn't have had a long time then to speculate upon the immortality of the soul. I would have possessed first-hand information. One can understand why, for their own protection, the Germans imposed their iron laws upon the Belgians with their terrible penalties. What is hard to understand is the long-suffering patience and self-restraint of the Belgians. Occasionally some high-spirited or high-strung fellow was no longer able to keep the lid on the volcano of hatred and rage seething within him. This blow-up brought down, not only upon his own head, but upon the whole community, the most hideous reprisals.

By the time my writing was completed the men were pretty well settled down for the night. On the outside the roaring of the Austrian guns, which for days had been bombarding their way into Antwerp, now became less constant; less and less frequently the hoarse commands of the officers, mingled with the rumbling of the automobiles, came up from the courtyard below. At midnight the only sounds were the groans and moans of the twisting sleepers and the measured tread of the sentry as he paced up and down the hall, his silhouette darkening at regular intervals the glass door at the end of our little room.

I was placed in a sort of adjoining closet with six others. A motley mixture indeed; a Russian, an American, four Belgians, and a German - all prisoners awaiting our sentences. As a last move, the German soldier guards sandwiched themselves into the open spaces on the floor, their long bayonets glistening in the electric light that blazed down upon us. The peasants had characteristically closed the windows to keep out the baneful night air. In the main room a drop-light with shade flung its radiance on a table and lit up the anxious faces of the few men gathered round it. It showed one poor fellow bolt upright, unspeaking, unmoving, his fixed white eyeballs staring into space, as though he would go stark mad. Those eyes have forever burned themselves into my brain, a pitiful protest against a mad, wild world at war.

Sleep was entirely out of the question with me. It wasn't the bad air or the hard floor or the snores of my comrades, but just plain cold fear. Now I possess an average amount of courage. Quite alone I walked in and out of Liége when the Germans were painting the skies red with the burning towns. My ribs were massaged all the way by ends of revolvers, whose owners demanded me to give forthwith my reasons for being there, they being sole arbiters of whether my reasons were good or bad. I got so used to a bayonet pointing into the pit of my stomach that it hardly looks natural in a vertical position.

But this was a thrust from a different quarter. In the open a man feels a sporting chance, at any rate, even if a bullet can beat him on the run; but cooped up within four walls he is paralyzed by his horrible helplessness. He feels that a military court reverses ordinary procedure, holding that it is better for nine innocent to suffer than for one guilty one to escape. He knows that his fate is in the hands of a tribunal from whose arbitrary decision there is no appeal, and that decision he knows may depend upon the whim of the commandant, to whom a poor breakfast or a bad night's sleep may give the wrong twist. The terrible uncertainty of it preys upon one's mind.

I certainly prayed that the commandant was getting a better night than mine, as I lay there staring up at the electric light with a hundred hates and fears pounding through my brain. "I'm a prisoner," was one thought. "Supposing the silence of the guns means that the Germans, beaten, are being pressed back into Brussels by the Allies. They may let us go. No, the Germans, maddened by defeat, might order us all to be shot," was one idea. "How does it feel to be blindfolded and stood up against a wall by a firing squad?" was another pleasant companion idea that kept vigil with me through the midnight hours. Then my fancies took a frenzied turn, "Suppose these be brutes of soldiers and they run us through, saying we were trying to escape."

"Escape!" The word no sooner leaped into my mind than an almost uncontrollable impulse to escape seized me, or at least I thought one had. I got upon my feet, observing that the two soldiers lying beside me on the floor were fast asleep and the guards at the outer door were nodding. I stepped over their sleeping forms and made a reconnoiter of the hallway. There in the semi-darkness stood seven soldiers of the Kaiser with their seven guns and their seven glistening bayonets.

Cold steel is not supposed to act as a soothing syrup; but one glance at those bayonets and my uncontrollable impulse utterly vanished. You will observe that the bayonet is continually cropping up in my story. It does, indeed. A bayonet looks far different from what it did on dress parade. Meet one in war, and its true significance first dawns upon you. It is not simply a decoration at the end of a rifle, but it is made to stick in a man's stomach and then be turned round; and when you realize that this particular one is made to stick in your particular stomach, it takes on a still different aspect.

I crawled back into my lair, resolved to seek for deliverance by mental means, rather than by physical; and as the first rays of light stole through the window I composed the following document to His Excellency:

The Officer who has the case of the American, Albert R. Williams, under supervision:

SIR:

As you seem willing to be fair in hearing my case, may I take the liberty this morning of addressing you upon my charge? I fear that I made but a feeble defense of myself yesterday; but when I was accused of offering much money for information relative to the movements of German troops, the accusation came so suddenly that I could only deny it. May I now offer a few observations upon this charge, the nature of which just begins to become dear to me?

In the first place, it was a sheer impossibility for me to offer "much money," because all I had was that which, as Mr. Van Hee knows, Mr. Fletcher gave me when I was left behind.

In the second place, were I a spy, I certainly would not be offering money in a voice loud enough to be heard by the several witnesses that you have ready to testify.

In the third place, while not attempting to impeach the character of my accuser, may I submit the fact that my own standing will be vouched for by His Excellency the Governor of Massachusetts, the President of the Pilgrim Amalgamated Associated Advertising Clubs of America, the chief Rabbi in the Rabbinate of New England, etc., etc.

These men will attest the utter absurdity of any such charge being made against me.

In the last place, may I suggest that the theory of an unintentional mistake throws the best light upon the case? For any conversation with my accuser was either in German or English. You know my German linguistic ability and the error that might be made there; and as for English, I challenge my accuser to understand three consecutive sentences in English.

I trust you will take these facts into account before sentence is passed upon me.

Respectfully yours,
ALBERT R. WILLIAMS.

By the time this was finished a stir in the courtyard below heralded the beginning of the day's activities. And what did this day hold in store for me!

CHAPTER IV
ROULETTE AND LIBERTY

O UR MORNING TOILET was completed with the aid of one small, flimsy towel for thirty of us. Hot water tinctured with coffee and milk was served from a bucket with two or three cups. Bread which had been saved from the previous day was brought forth from pockets and hiding-places, and for some unaccountable reason a piece of good butter was brought in. Apparently the Germans were trying to escape the stigma of mistreating or underfeeding their prisoners.

Orders were given to get ready to move out. After an hour, they were changed to "Clean up the room." When we had accomplished this, an inspecting officer entered and began to sniff and snort until his eyes fairly blazed with wrath, and then in a torrent of words he expressed his private and official opinion of us. So fast and freely did his language flow that I couldn't catch all the compliments he showered upon us; but *"Verdammte!" "Donnerwetter!"* and *"Schwein!"* were stressed frequently enough for me to retain a distinct memory of the same. One did not have to be a German linguist to get the drift of his remarks.

They had an electric effect upon the prisoners, who with one accord got busy picking up microscopic and invisible bits from the floor. To see these men crawling around upon their stomachs must have been highly gratifying to His Self-inflated Highness. The highly gratifying thing to myself now is the fact that I did not do any crawling, but sat stolidly in my chair and stared back at him, letting my indignation get enough the better of my discretion even to sneer - at least I persuade myself now that I did. Outside of this little act of gallantry I am heartily ashamed of my conduct at the German Staff Headquarters. It was too acquiescent and obsequious for some of those bureaucrats rough-riding it over those helpless, long-suffering, beaten Belgians.

Having called us *"Schwein,"* at high noon they brought in the swill.

It was a gray, putrid-looking mess in a big, battered bucket. They told us that it came dried in bags and all that was necessary was to mix the contents with hot water. The mixture was put up in 1911 and guaranteed to keep for 20 years. It looked as though it might have already forfeited on its guarantee. There was nothing to serve it with, and search of the room uncovered no implements of attack. Our discomfiture furnished a young soldier with much entertainment.

"Nothing to eat your stew with? Well, just stand on that table there and dive right into the bucket."

He was quite carried away with his own witticism, so that in sheer good nature he went and returned with six soup plates which were covered over with a thick grease quite impervious to cold water. I had my misgivings about the mess and dreaded its steaming odors. At last I summoned up courage and approached the bucket, using my fingers in lien of a clothes-pin as a defense for my olfactory nerves. A surprise was in store for me; its palatability and quality were quite the opposite of its appearance. While I wouldn't enjoy that stew outside of captivity, and while the Brussels men refused in any way to succumb to its charm, it was at least very nutritious and furnished the strength to keep fighting.

But it is hard to battle against the blues, especially when all one's comrades capitulate to them. Each man vied with the other in radiating a blue funk, until the air was as thick as a London fog.

Picture, if you will, the scene. By a fine irony, the books on the shelves were on international law, and by a finer irony the book in green binding that caught my eye as it stood out from the black array of volumes was R. Dimmont's "The Origins of Belgian Neutrality." The Belgians who were enjoying the peculiar blessings of that neutrality were sprawled over the floor or pacing restlessly up and down the room, or, in utter despair, buried their heads in their arms flung out across the table.

About three o'clock the name "Herr Peters" was called. He had been found guilty of mumbling to his comrades that their captain was pushing them too hard in an advance. One could believe the charge, for, as his name was called, he was sullen and unconcerned. "You are sentenced to imprisonment at hard labor in a fortress. You must go at once."

He muttered in an undertone something about "being luckier in prison in winter than out there on the cold, freezing ground," and, flinging his knapsack upon his shoulder, lumbered off. In how many such hearts is there this sullen revolt against the military system, and how much of a factor will it be to reckon with in the future?

There were four prisoners quite separated from the rest of us. It was said that they were sentenced to be shot. I am not sure that they were; but we were strictly forbidden any intercourse with them. They were the most crestfallen, terror-stricken lot of men that ever I had laid eyes upon, and at four o'clock they were led away by a cordon of soldiers. There was enough mental suggestion about it to plunge the room into a deep silence. It was oppressive.

At last Obels, the reporter, walked over and asked me if there were proofs of the immortality of the soul, excusing himself by saying that up to this time he had never had any particular time nor reason for reflection on this subject. That was the only psychological blunder that he made. However, it at last broke the heavy, painful silence, and we speculated together, instead of singly, how it might feel to have immortal bliss thrust upon us from the end of a German musket.

I related to him my experience of the previous week. Some war photographers wanted a picture of a spy shot. I had volunteered to play the part of a spy, and, after being blindfolded, was led over against a wall, where a Belgian squad leveled their rifles at me. I assured him that the sensation was by no means terrible; but he would not be comforted. Death itself he wouldn't mind so much, if he could have found it in the open fighting gladly for his country; but it seemed a blot on his good name to be shot for just snooping around the German lines.

On the whole, after weighing all the pros and cons, we decided that our pronounced aversion to being shot had purely an altruistic origin. It was a wicked, shameful loss to the human race. That point was very clear to us. But there was the arrant stupidity of the Germans to be reckoned with. They have such a distorted sense of real values. Rummaging through my pockets during these reflections, I fished up an advertising folder out of a comer where I had tucked it when it was presented to me by Dr. Morse. The outside read, "How We Lost Our Best Customer." Mechanically I opened it, and there, staring back at me from big black borders on the inside, were the two words, "HE DIED."

These ruminations upon matters spiritual were interrupted by the strains from a brass band which went crashing by, while ten thousand hobnailed boots of the regiment striking the pavements in unison beat out time like a trip-hammer.

"Perhaps the Germans are leaving Brussels," whispered a companion; "and wouldn't we grow wild or faint or crazy to see those guards drop away and we should find ourselves free men again!"

The passing music had a jubilating effort upon our guards, who paraded gayly up and down the room. One simple, good-hearted fellow harangued us in a bantering way, pointing out our present sorry plight as evidence of the sad mistake we had made in not being born in Germany. He felt so happy that he took a little collection from us, and in due time returned with some bread and chocolate and soda water. But even the soda water, as if adjusting itself to the spiritlessness of the prisoners, refused to effervesce. The music had by contrast seemed only to increase the general depression.

Only one free spirit soared above his surroundings. He was a young Belgian - Ernest de Burgher by name - a kindly light amidst the encircling gloom. He took everything in life with a smile. I am sure that if death as a spy had been ordered for him at the door, he would have met that with the same happy, imperturbable expression. He had quite as much reason as I, if not more, for joining our gloom-party. He, too, was waiting sentence. For six days his wild, untamed spirit had been cabined in these walls; but he had been born a humorist, and even in bonds he sought to play the clown. He went through contortions, pitched coins against himself, and staggered around the room with a soda-water bottle at his lips, imitating a drunkard. But ours was a tough house even for his irrepressible spirit to play to. Despite all his efforts, we sat around like a convention of corpses, and only once did his comic spirit succeed.

One prisoner sunk down in a comatose condition in his chair, as though his last drop of strength and life had oozed away. Now de Burgher was one of those who can resist anything but temptation. He stole over and tied the man's legs to his chair. Then he got a German soldier to tap the hapless victim on the shoulder. Roused from his stupor to see the soldier standing over him like a messenger of doom, the poor fellow turned ashen pale. He sprang to his feet, but the chair bound to his legs tripped him up and he fell sprawling on the floor. He apparently regarded the chair as some sort of German infernal machine clutching him, and he lay there wrestling with his inanimate antagonist as though it were a demon. As soon as the victim understood the joke he joined in the burst of merriment that ran round the room; but it was of short duration. The gloom got us again, despite all that de Burgher could do, and finally he succumbed to the prevailing atmosphere and gave us up as a bad job.

He was a diminutive fellow, battered and rather the worse for wear. Ever shall I think of him not only as the happy-souled, but as the great-souled. My introduction into the room was at the point of a steel bayonet. With him, that served me far better than any gilt-edged introduction of high estate. He didn't know what crime was charged against me, but he felt that it must have been a sacrifice for Belgium's sake. The fact that I was *persona non grata* to the Germans was a lien upon his sympathy, and gave me high rank with him at once.

He instinctively divined my feelings of fear and loneliness, and straightway set out to make me his ward, his comrade, and his master.

Never shall I forget how, during that long night in prison, he crawled over and around the recumbent forms to where I lay upon the floor courting sleep in vain. I was frightened by this maneuver, but he smiled and motioned me to silence. Reaching up beneath my blanket, he unlaced one shoe and then the other. At first I really thought that he was going to steal them, but the reaction from the day had set in and I was too tired and paralyzed to make any protest. Laying the shoes one side, he remarked, "That will ease your feet." Then stripping off his coat and rolling it into a bundle, he placed it as a pillow beneath my head.

A great, big hulking American, treated tenderly by this little Belgian, how could I keep the tears from my eyes? And as they came welling up - tears of appreciation for the generous fineness of his spirit - he took them to be tears of grief, brought on by thoughts of home and friends and all those haunting memories. But he was equal to the occasion.

In a little vacant space he made a circle of cigarettes and small Belgian coins. In the center he placed a small box, and on it laid a ruler. "This is the roulette wheel at Monte Carlo, and you are the rich American," he whispered, and with a snap of the finger he spun the ruler round. Whenever it stopped, he presented me my prize with sundry winkings and chucklings, interrupted by furtive glances towards the door.

Rouge-et-noir upon a prison floor! To him existence was such a game - red life or black death, as the fates ordained. His spirit was contagious, and I found myself smiling through my tears. When he saw his task accomplished, gathering in his coins, he crawled away.

His was a restless spirit. Only once did I see him steadfastly quiet. That was the next morning, when he sat with his eyes fixed upon an opening in the shutter. He insisted upon my taking his seat, and adjusting my angle of vision properly. There, framed in a window across the forbidden courtyard, was a pretty girl watering flowers. She was indeed a distracting creature, and de Burgher danced around me with unfeigned glee. His previous experience with Americans had evidently led him to believe that we were all connoisseurs in pretty girls. I tried valiantly to uphold our national reputation, but my thoughts at the time were much more heavenly than even that fair apparition framed in the window, and I fear I disappointed de Burgher by my lack of enthusiasm.

My other comrade, Constance Staes, must not be forgotten. For some infraction of the new military regulations he had been hustled off to prison, but he, too, was born for liberty, a free- ranging spirit that fetters could never bind. He made me see the Belgian soul that would never be subservient to German rule. The Germans can be overlords in Belgium only when such spirits have either emigrated or have been totally exterminated.

To Constance Staes every rule was a challenge. That's the reason he had been put in jail. He had trespassed on forbidden way in front of the East Station. Here in prison smoking was forbidden. So Staes, with one eye upon the listless guard, would slip beneath a blanket, take a pull at his cigarette, and come up again as innocent as though he had been saying his prayers. I refused the offer of a pull at his cigarette, but not the morsel of white bread which he drew from behind a picture and shared with me. That bread, broken and shared between us in that upper room, is to me an eternal sacrament. It fed my body hunger then; never shall it cease to feed the hunger of my soul.

Whenever temptation to play the cynic or think meanly of my fellow-man shall come, my mind will hark back to those two unpretending fellows and bow in reverence before the selflessness and immensity of the human soul. Needing bread, they gave it freely away; needing strength, they poured themselves out unsparingly; needing encouragement, they became the ministers thereof. For not to me alone, but to ally they played this role of servant, priest, and comforter.

As I write these lines I wonder where their spirits are now. Speeded thence, they may have already made the next world richer by their coming. I do not know that; but I do know that they have made my soul infinitely richer by their sojourn here; I do not know whether they were Catholic or Atheist, but I do know how truly the Master of all souls could say to these two brave little Belgians: "When I was an hungered, ye gave me food; when I was thirsty, ye gave me drink; when I was a stranger, ye took me in; when I was sick and in prison, ye visited me."

The prison is the real maker of democracy. I saw that clearly when, at five o'clock, joy came marching into the room. It was an officer who was its herald with the simple words, "The theater manager is free." That was a trumpet blast annihilating all rank and caste. The manager, forgetting his office and his dignity, and embracing with his right arm a peasant and with his left an artisan, danced round the room in a delirium of delight. Twenty men were at one time besieging him to grasp his handy and tears, not rhetorically, but actually, were streaming down their faces - Russian, German, Belgian, and American, high and low, countrymen and citymen, smocked and frocked. We were fused altogether in the common emotion of joy and hope. For hope was now rampant. "If one man can be liberated," we argued, "why not another? Perhaps the General was thus giving vent to a temporary vein of good humor." Each man figured that he might be the fortunate one upon whom this good luck would alight.

At five-thirty there was much murmuring in the corridor, and presently my *Ehrenwort* lad of the previous night came bursting into the room, crying, "The American! The American!" I do not have to describe the thrill of joy that those words shot through me; but I wish that I might do justice to the beaming face of my young officer friend. I am sure that I could not have looked more radiant than he did when, almost like a mother, he led me forth to greet de Leval and two other assistants from the American Ambassador. Now de Leval is not built on any sylph-like plan, but he looked to me then like an ethereal being from another world - the angel who opened the prison door.

I presumed that I was to walk away without further ado; but not so easy. We proceeded into another office, where the whole assemblage was standing. I have no idea who the high superior officer was; but he held in his hand a blue book which contained a long report of my case, with all the documents except the defense I had written. Again I was cross-examined, and my papers were carefully passed upon one by one.

One they could not or would not overlook, and to it throughout all this last examination they kept perpetually referring. When I had made my thirty-seven-mile journey into Liége on August 20, I had secured this paper at Maastricht signed by the Dutch and German authorities. Over the Dutch seal were the words, "To the passing over the boundary into Belgian-Germany of Mr. Albert Williams there exists on the part of the undersigned no objection. Signed, The Commissioner of Police Souten." Over the German seal were the words, "At the Imperial German Vice-Consulate the foregoing signature is hereby attested to be that of Souten, the Police Commissioner of Maastricht." For this beautifully non-committal affair I had delivered up six marks. I would have cheerfully paid six hundred to disown it now.

"What explanation is there for his possession of that paper?" asked the General sternly.

De Leval pleaded cleverly, dilating upon the natural inquisitiveness and roaming disposition of the American race.

"I know what the *Wanderlust* is," said the General, "but I fail to understand the peculiar desire of this man to travel only in dangerous and forbidden war zones.

"In the second place," the General continued, "there is no doubt that he has made some remark to the effect that in the long run Germany cannot win. That was overheard by an officer in a café and is undeniable. The other charges we will for the time waive," said the General, drawing himself up with a fine hauteur. "But his identifying evidence is very flimsy. Can you produce any better?"

Suddenly I bethought me of the gold watch in my pocket. It was a presentation from some two hundred people of small means in an industrial district in Boston. Three of the aides successively and successfully damaged their thumbnails in their eagerness to pry open the back cover. That is a source of considerable satisfaction to me now; but it was embarrassing in that delicate situation when my fate hung almost by a thread, and a trifle could delay my release for days. If the General damaged his own thumb on it, I feel sure that I would have been remanded back to prison. But, luckily, the cover sprang open and revealed to the eyes the words: "From friends at Maverick."

De Leval adroitly turned this to the best advantage. It was the last straw. The General capitulated. Walking over into the adjoining room, he wrote on the blue folder: *"Er ist frei gelassen."* I would give lots for those folders; but, though safety was by no means certain, I found I yet had nerve enough to take a venture. When I was bidden to pick up my papers strewn across the desk, I tried my best to gather in some of the other documents. Besides the copies of the letter I wrote to the Ambassador the only thing I got on my case was this letter, written by Mr. Whitlock to Baron von de Lancken, the official German representative in charge of the dealings with the American Embassy. It has the well-known Whitlock straight-from-the-shoulder point and brevity to it.

Bruxelles, le 29 Septembre, 1914.

Excellence:

J'apprends à l'instant que Mr. Williams, citoyen Américain résidente à l'Hôtel Métropole, aurait été arrêté lundi par les Autorités allemande.

Pour le cas où il n'aurait pas encore êté mis en liberté, je vous saurais gré de me faire connaître les raisons de cette arrestation, et de me donner le moyen de communiquer aussitôt avec lui, pour pourvoir eventuellement lui foumir toute protection dont it pourrait avoir besoin.

Veuillez agréer, Excellence, la nouvelle assurance de ma haute considération.

(S) Brand Whitlock.

A Son Excellence Monsieur le Baron
von der Lancken, Bruxelles.

Before my final liberation I was escorted into the biggest and busiest office of all.

Here I was given an *Erlaubnis* to travel by military train through Liége into Germany, and from there on out by way of Holland. The destination that I had in mind was Ghent, but passing through the lines thereto was forbidden. Instead of going directly the thirty miles in three hours, I must go around almost a complete circle, about three hundred miles in three days. But nothing could take the edge off my joy. A strange exhilaration and a wild desire to celebrate possessed me. With such a mood I had not hitherto been sympathetic; on the contrary, I had been much grieved by the sundry manifestations of what I deemed a base spirit in certain Belgians. One of them had said, "Just wait until the Allies' army comes marching into Brussels! Oh, then I am going out on one glorious drank!" In the light of the splendid sacrifices of his fellow-Belgians, this struck me as a shocking degradation of the human spirit.

I could not then understand such a viewpoint. But I could now. In the removal of the long abnormal tension one's pent-up spirits seek out an equally abnormal channel for expression. I, too, felt like an uncaged spirit suddenly let loose. I didn't get drunk, but I very nearly got arrested again. In my headlong ecstasy I was deaf to the warnings of a German guard saying, "Passage into this street is forbidden." I checked myself just in time, and in chastened spirit made my way back to the Métropole.

Three times I was offered the prohibited Antwerp papers that had been smuggled into the city and once the London *Times* for twenty-five cents. The war price for this is said often to have run up to as many dollars.

An English woman, or at any rate a woman with a beautiful English accent, opened a conversation with the remark that she was going directly through to Ghent on the following day and that she knew how to go right through the German lines. That was precisely the way that the Germans had just forbidden me to go. But this accomplice (if such she was) got no rise out of me. To all intents I was stone-deaf. Compared to me, she would have found the Sphinx garrulous indeed. She may have been as harmless as a dove but, after my escapade, I wouldn't have talked to my own mother without a written permit from the military governor. The Kaiser himself would have found it hard work breaking through my cast-iron spy-proof armor of formality. I had good reason, too, not to let down the bars, for I was trailed by the spy-hunters. Not until ten days later when I passed over the Holland border did I feel release from their vigilant eyes. My key at the Métropole was never returned to me and I know that my room was searched once, if not twice, after my return to the hotel.

It would be interesting to see how all this tallies with the official report of my case in the archives at Berlin. Perhaps some of these surmises have shot far wide of the mark Javert, for instance, may not be a direct descendant of the ancient Inquisitor who had charge of the rack and the thumb screws, as I believed. In his own home town he may be a sort of mild-mannered schoolmaster and probably is highly astounded as well as gratified to find himself cast as the villain in this piece. Perhaps I may have been at other times in far greater danger. I do not know these things. All I know is that this is a true and faithful transcript of the feelings and sights that came crowding in upon me in that most eventful day and night.

PART II
ON FOOT WITH THE GERMAN ARMY

CHAPTER V
THE GRAY HORDES OUT
OF THE NORTH

T HE OUTBREAK OF the Great War found me in Europe as a
general tourist, and not in the capacity of war-correspondent.
Hitherto I had essayed a much less romantic rôle in life, belonging rather
to the crowd of uplifters who conduct the drab and dreary battle with
the slums. The futility of most of these schemes for badgering the poor
makes one feel at times that these battles are shams and unavailing. This
is depressing. It is thrilling, then, suddenly to acquire the glamorous title
of war-correspondent, and to have before one the prospect of real and
actual battles.

Commissioned thus and desiring to live up to the code and
requirement of the office, I naturally opined that war-correspondents
rushed immediately into the thick of the fight. Later I discovered what a
mistake that was. Only very young and green ones do so. The seasoned
correspondent is inclined to view the whole affair more dispassionately
and with a larger perspective. But being of the verdant variety, I naturally
figured that if the Germans were smashing down through Belgium onto
Liége that that was where I should be. By entering gingerly through the
back door of Holland, I planned to join them in their march down the
Meuse River.

To The Hague came descriptions of the hordes pressing down out
of the north through the fire-swept, blood-drenched plain of northern
Belgium. This could be seen from the Dutch frontier at Maastricht. But
passage thereto was interdicted by the military authorities. Ambassador
Van Dyke's efforts were unavailing. Possessing a red-card, I enlisted the
help of Troelstra, the socialist leader of the Netherlands.

He had just returned from an audience with the Queen. The

government, seeking to rally all classes to face a grave crisis, was paying court to the labor leaders. Accordingly, the war department, at Troelstra's behest, received me with a handsome show of deference. I was escorted from one gold-laced officer to another. Each one smiled kindly, listened attentively and regretted exceedingly that the granting of the desired permission lay outside his own particular jurisdiction. They were polite, ingratiating, obsequious even, but quite unanimous. At the end I came out by the same door wherein I went - minus a permission.

Up till now my progress through the fringes of the war zone had been in defiance of all orders and advice. Having failed here officially, I took the matter in my own hands. Finding a seat in a military train, I stuck steadfastly by it so long as our general direction was south. At Eindhoven hunger compelled me to alight. As I was stepping up to the hotel-bar, I felt a tap on my shoulder and some one in excellent English said:

"You are under suspicion, sir. Follow me. Don't look around. Don't get excited. If you are all right you don't need to get excited; if you aren't it won't do you any good to get excited."

With this running fire of comment lie led me into a side-room where a half-hour's examination satisfied him of my good intent. Without further untoward incident I came to Maastricht in Limbourg. Limbourg is the name of the narrow strip of Dutch territory which runs down between Germany and Belgium. At one place this tongue of land is but a few miles wide. If the Germans could have marched their troops directly across this they might have been spared the two weeks' slaughter at the forts of Liége and Paris, in all probability, would have fallen before them. It was a great temptation to the Germans. That's the reason the Dutch troops had been massed here by the tens of thousands - to prevent Germany succumbing to that temptation.

At our approach to the great Meuse bridge an officer shouted into each compartment:

"Every window closed. All cigars and pipes extinguished."

"Why?" we asked.

"The bridge is mined with explosives and a stray spark might set them off," a soldier informed us.

The first German attempt to set foot on the bridge would be the signal for sending the great structure crashing skywards.

The end of the run was Maastricht, now become a town of crucial interest. It was like a city besieged. Barricades of barbed wire and paving stones ripped from street ran everywhere. Iron rails and ties blocked the exits and the small cannon disconcertingly thrust their nozzles down upon one out of the windows.

I lingered here long enough to secure a carriage and with it made quick time across the harvest fields. We were soon up on the little hill back of Mesch. The sun was sinking and for the first time war, in all its terrible spectacular splendor, smote me hard. From the hill at my feet there stretched away a great plain filled with a dense mass of German soldiery. One could scarcely believe that there were men there so well did their gray-green coats blend with the landscape. One would think that they were indeed a part of it, could he not feel the atmosphere vibrant with the mass personality of the myriad warriors tramping down the crops of the peasants. In the rear the commissariat vans and artillery still came lumbering up, while in the very front pranced the horses of the dreaded Uhlans, who looked with contempt, I imagined, on the Dutch soldiers as they stood there with the warning that here was Netherlands soil.

In the fighting German and Belgian troops had already been pushed up against this line. Here they were greeted with the challenge: "Lay down your arms. This is the neutral soil of Holland." Thus many were interned until the end of the war.

As even darkened into night, the endless plain became stippled over with points of flame from countless campfires. There were beauty and mystery in this vast menace sweeping the soul of the onlooker now with horror, and now with admiration. There was a terrible background to the spectacle - glowing red and luminous. It was made of the still blazing towns of Mouland and Visé, burned to the ground by order of the invaders. The fire had been set as a warning to the inhabitants round about. They were taking the warning and hastening by the thousands across the border into Holland, their only haven of safety.

When we drove down from the hill into Eysden, we were in the midst of these peasants, fleeing before the red wrath rolling up into the sky. They came shambling in with a few possessions on which they had hurriedly laid their hands, singly or in families, a pitiful procession of the disinherited.

Some of the men were moaning as they marched along, but most of them were taking it with the tragic oxlike resignation of the peasant, stupefied more than terrified, puzzled why these soldiers were coming down into their quiet little villages to fight out their quarrels. The women were crying out to Mary and all the saints. Indeed all the little crosses along the waysides or in the walls were decked with flowers in gratitude for what had been spared them. In most cases it was little more than their lives, their brood of children, and their dogs that followed on.

My driver finally landed me in a shack on the outskirts of Eysden, which boasted the name of a hotel It had the worst bed I ever slept in, and the only window was a hole in the roof.

I wandered out among the unfortunates, now herded in halls and schools and packed in the homes of the friendly villagers. They were full of the weirdest tales of loot and murder. And while there were no tears in their eyes there was tragedy in their voices.

"It would be worth while getting over to the sources and verifying the truth of these stories," I remarked.

"A sheer impossibility, and only a fool would want to go," was one laconic commentary.

I kept up my plaint and was overheard by Souten, head of the Limbourg police.

"American, aren't you?" he interjected.

"Well, I have done more work here in the last five days than I did in the five years that I lived in New York. Had the best time in my life there. If you want to go sight-seeing in Belgium, take this paper and get it counter-signed at the German consulate. It's the only one I've given out to-day."

I hurried off to the consul who, in return for six marks, duly impressed it with the German seal. Later on I would gladly have given six hundred marks to disown it.

"Of course you understand that this is simply a paper issued by the civil authorities," said the consul, as he passed it out. "Use it at your own risk. If you go ahead and get shot by the military authorities, don't come back and blame us."

I promised that I wouldn't and was off again to my hotel.

As darkness deepened, with two Hollanders come to view the havoc of war, I sat on the stoop of our little inn. A great rumbling of cannon came from the direction of Tongres. A sentry shot rang out on the frontier just across the river which flowed not ten rods away. This was the Meuse, which ran red with the blood of the combatants, and from which the natives drew the floating corpses to the shore. Now its gentle lapping on the stones mingled with the subdued murmur of our talk. In such surroundings my new friends regaled me with stories of pillage and murder which the refugees had been bringing in from across the border. All this produced a distinct depreciation in the value that I had hitherto attached to my permit to go visiting across that border. Souten's declarations of friendship for America had been most voluble. It began dawning on me that his apparently generous and impulsive action might bear a different interpretation than unadulterated kindness.

At this juncture, I remember, a great light flared suddenly up. It was one of the fans of a wind-mill fired by the Germans. In the foreground we could see the soldiers standing like so many gray wolves silhouetted against the red flames. In that light it did seem that motives other than pure affection might have prompted the Police Commissioner's action. The hectic sleep of the night was broken by the endless clatter of the hoofs of the German cavalry pushing south.

My courage rose, however, with the rising sun. In the morning I climbed to the lookout on the hill. The hosts had vanished. A trampled, smoldering fire-blackened land lay before me. But there was the lure of the unknown. I walked down to where the great Netherlands flag proclaimed neutral soil. The worried Dutch pickets honored the signature of Souten and with one step I was over the border into Belgium, now under German jurisdiction. The helmeted soldiers across the way were a distinct disappointment. They looked neither fierce nor fiery. In fact, they greeted me with a smile. They were a bit puzzled by my paper, but the seal seemed *echt-Deutsch* and they pronounced it *"gut, sehr gut."* I explained that I wished to go forwards to Liége.

"Was it possible?"

For answer they shrugged their shoulders.

"Was it dangerous?"

"Not in the least," they assured me.

The Germans were right. It was not dangerous - that is, for the Germans. By repeatedly proclaiming the everlasting friendship of Germany and America, and passing out some chocolate, I made good friends on the home base. They charged me only not to return after sundown, giving point to their advice by relating how, on the previous night, they had shot down a peasant woman and her two children who, under the cloak of darkness, sought to scurry past the sentinels. They told this with a genuine note of grief in their voices. So, with a hearty hand-shake and wishes for the best of luck, they waved adieu to me as I went swinging out on the highroad to Liége.

Chapter VI
In the Black Wake
of the War

A HALF-MILE and I came for the first time actually face to face with the wastage of war. There was what once was Mouland, the little village I had seen burning the night before. The houses stood roofless and open to the sky, like so many tombstones over a departed people. The whitewashed outer walls were all shining in the morning sun. Inside they were charred black, or blazing yet with coals from the fire still slowly burning its way through wood and plaster. Here and there a house had escaped the torch.

By some miracle in the smashed window of one of these houses a bright red geranium blossomed. It seemed to cry for water, but I dared not turn aside, for fear of a bullet from a lurking sentry. In another a sewing-machine of American make testified to the thrift and progressiveness of one household. In the last house as I left the village a rocking-horse with its head stuck through the open door smiled its wooden smile, as if at any rate it could keep good cheer even though the roofs might fall.

My road now wound into the open country; and I was heartily glad of it, for the hedges and the houses at Mouland provided fine coverts for prowling German foragers or for Belgians looking for revenge. Dead cows and horses and dogs with their sides ripped open by bullets lay along the wayside. The roads were deep printed with the hoofs of the cavalry. The grain-fields were flattened out. Nine little crosses marked the place where nine soldiers of the Kaiser fell.

This smiling countryside, teeming with one of the densest populations in the world, had been stripped dean of every inhabitant. Along the wasted way not the sign of a civilian, or for that matter even a soldier, was to be seen. I was glad even of the presence of a pig which, with her litter, was enjoying the unwonted pleasure of rooting out her morning meal in a rich flower-garden. She did not reciprocate, however, with any such fellow feeling. Perhaps of late she had seen enough of the doings of the genus homo. Surveying me as though I had been the author of all this destruction, she gave a frightened snort and plunged into a nearby thicket.

I craved companionship of any living creature to break the spell of death and silence. I was destined to have the wish gratified in abundance. Fifteen minutes brought me to the outskirts of Visé, and there, coming over the hills and wending their way down to the river, were two long lines of German soldiers escorting wagons of the artillery and the commissariat. They came slowly and noiselessly trudging on and I was upon them as they crossed the main road before I realized it. The men were covered with dust; so were the horses. The wagons were in their somber paint of gray. There was something ominous and threatening in the long sullen line which wound down over the hill. The soldiers were evidently tired with the tedious uneventful march, and the drivers were goaded to irritability by the difficulty of the descent. Could I have retreated I would have done so with joy and would never have stopped until my feet were set on Holland soil.

But I dared not do it As the train came to a stop, I started bravely across the road. A soldier, dropping his gun from his shoulder, cried:

"Halt!"

"Is this the way to Visé?" I asked.

"Perhaps it is," he replied, "but what do you want in Visé?"

As he spoke, he kept edging up, pointing his bayonet directly at me. A bayonet will never look quite the same to me again. Total retreat, as I remarked, was out of the question. My inward anatomy, however, did the next best thing. As the bayonet point came pressing for- ward, my stomach retired backward. I could feel it distinctly making efforts to crawl behind my spine. At my first word of German his face relaxed. Ditto my stomach.

"You are an American," he said. "Well, good for that. I don't know what we would have done were you a Belgian. Our orders are to suffer no Belgian in this whole district."

Then he began an apologia which I heard repeated identically again and again, as if it were learned by rote: "The Germans had peacefully entered the land; boiling hot water was showered on them from upper stories; they were shot at from houses and hedges; many soldiers had thus been killed; the wells had been poisoned. Such acts of treachery had necessarily brought reprisals, etc., etc." It was the defense so regularly served up to neutrals that we learned in time to reproduce it almost word for word ourselves.

We all rise to the glorification of suffering little Belgium. Whatever brief we may hold for her though, we ought not to picture even her peasant people as a mild, meek and inoffensive lot. That isn't the sort of stuff out of which her dogged and continuing resistance was wrought. That isn't the mettle which for two weeks stopped up the German tide before the Liége forts, giving the allies two weeks to mobilize, and all they had asked the Belgians for was two or three days of grace. But before the German avalanche hurled itself on Liége it was this peasant population which bore the first brunt of the battle.

A mistake in the branching roads brought this home to me. I turned off in the direction of Verviers and was puzzled to see the road on either side strewn with tree-trunks, their sprawling limbs still green with leaves. It was along this highway that the invaders first entered Belgium. The peasants, turning their axes loose on the poplars and the royal elms that lined the road, had filled it with a tangle of interlocking limbs.

The Imperial army arrived with cannon which could smash a fort to pieces as though it were made of blue china, but of what avail were these against such yielding obstructions? Maddened that these shambling creatures of the soil should delay the military promenade through this little land, officers rushed out and held their pistols at the heads of the offenders, threatening to blow their brains out if they did not speedily clear the way. Many a peasant did not live to see his house go up in flames - his dwelling dyed by his own blood was now turned into a funeral pyre. These were the first sacrificial offerings of Belgium on the altar of her independence.

I now entered Visé, or rather what once had been the little city of Visé. It was almost completely annihilated and its three thousand inhabitants scattered. Through the mass of smoking ruins I pushed, with the paving-stones still hot beneath my feet. Quite unawares I ran full tilt into a group of soldiers, looking as ugly and dirty as the ruins amongst which they were prowling.

The green-gray field-uniform is a remarkable piece of obliterative coloration. I had seen it blend with grass and trees, but in this instance it fitted in so well with the stones and debris they were poking over that I was right amongst them without warning. They straightened up with a sudden start and scowled at me. Hollanders and Belgians had faithfully assured me that such marauding bands would shoot at sight. Here was an excellent test-case. Three hundred marks, a gold watch and a lot of food which crammed my pockets would be their booty.

I took the initiative with the bland inquiry, "What are you hunting for, corpses?"

"No," they responded, pointing to their mouths and stomachs, "awful hungry. Hunting something to eat."

I bade a mental farewell to my food-supplies as I emptied out my pockets before these ravagers. I expected everything to be grabbed with a summary demand for more. From these despoilers of a countryside I was ready for any sort of a manifestation - any, except the one that I received. With one accord they refused to take any of my provisions. I recovered from my surprise sufficiently to understand that they were thanking me for my good will while they were constantly reiterating:

"It is your food and you will need every bit of it."

In the name of *camaraderie* I persuaded each to take a piece of bread and chocolate. They received this offering with profound gratitude. With much cautioning and many solemn *Auf Wiedersehens* bestowed upon me, I was off again.

Below Visé an entirely new vista opened to me. Tens of thousands of soldiers were marching over the pontoon bridges already flung across the river. Perhaps five hundred more were engaged in building a steel bridge which seemed to be a hurried but remarkable piece of engineering. It was replacing the old structure which had been dynamited by the Belgians, and which now lay a tangled mass of wreckage in the river.

For the next eight miles to Jupilles the country was quite as much alive as the first four miles were dead. It was swarming with the military. Through all the gaps in the hills above the River Meuse the German army came pouring down like an enormous tidal wave - a tidal wave with a purpose, viz: to fling itself against the Allies arranged in battle line at Namur, and with the overwhelming mass of numbers to smash that line to bits and sweep on resistlessly into Paris. I thought of the Blue and Bed wall of French and English down there awaiting this Gray-Green tide of Teutons.

By the hundreds of thousands they were coming; patrols of cavalry clattering along, the hoof -beats of the chargers coming with regular cadence on the hard roads; silent moving riders mounted on bicycles, their guns strapped on their backs; armored automobiles rambling slowly on, but taking the occasional spaces which opened in the road with a hollow roaring sound and at a terrific pace; individual horsemen galloping up and down the road with their messages, and the massed regiments of dust-begrimed men marching endlessly by.

I was glad to have the spell which had been woven on me broken by strains of music from a wayside café, or rather the remains of a café, for the windows had been demolished and wreckage was strewn about the door, but the piano within had survived the ravages. Though it was sadly out of tune, the officer, seated on a beer keg, was evoking a noise from its battered keys, and to its accompaniment some soldiers were bawling lustily:

"Deutschland, Deutschland über Alles!"

The only other music that echoed up along those river cliffs came from a full-throated Saxon regiment.

Evidently the Belgians from Visé to Liége had not roused the ire of the invaders as furiously as had the natives on the other side of Visé.

They had as a whole established more or less friendly relations with the alien hosts.

On the other side of Visé nothing had availed to stay the wrath of the Germans. Flags of truce made of sheets and pillow-cases and white petticoats were hung out on poles and broom handles; but many of these houses before which they hung had been burned to the ground as had the others.

One Belgian had sought for his own benefit to conciliate the Germans, and as the Kaiser's troops at the turn of the road came upon his house, there was the Kaiser's emblem with the double-headed eagle raised to greet them. The man had nailed it high up in an apple tree, that they might not mistake his attitude of trading disloyalty to his own country, hoping so to save his home. But let it be said to the credit of the Germans, that they had shown their contempt for this treachery by razing this house to the ground, and the poor fellow has lost his earthly treasures along with his soul.

I now came upon some houses that were undamaged and showed signs of life therein. Below Argenteau there was a vine-covered cottage before which stood a peasant woman guarding her little domain. Her weapon was not a rifle but several buckets of water and a pleasant smile. I ventured to ask how she used the water. She had no time to explain, for at that very moment a column of soldiers came slowly plodding down the dusty road. She motioned me away as though she would free herself from whatever stigma my presence might incur. A worried look clouded her face, as though she were saying to herself: "I know that we have been spared so far by all the brigands which have gone by, but perhaps here at last is the band that has been appointed to wipe us out." This water, then, was a peace-offering, a plea for mercy.

As soon as the soldiers looked her way she put a smile on her face, but it ill concealed her anxiety. She pointed invitingly to her pails. At the sight of the water a thirsty soldier here and there would break from the ranks, rush to the pails, take the proffered cup, and hastily swallow down the cooling draught. Then returning the cup to the woman, he would rush back again to his place in the ranks. Perhaps a dozen men removed their helmets, and, extracting a sponge from the inside, made signs to the woman to pour water on it; then, replacing the sponge in the helmet, marched on refreshed and rejoicing.

A mounted officer, spying this little oasis, drew rein and gave the order to halt. The troopers, very wearied by the long forced march, flung themselves down upon the grass while the officer's horse thrust his nose deep into the pail and greedily sucked the water up. More buckets were being continually brought out. Some of them must surely have been confiscated from her neighbors who had fled. The officer, dismounting, sought to hold converse with his hostess, but even with many signs it proved a failure. They both laughed heartily together, though her mirth I thought a bit forced.

I do not remember witnessing any finer episode in all the war than that enacted in this region where the sky was red with flames from the neighbors' houses, and the lintels red with blood from their veins. A frail little soul with only spiritual weapons, she fought for her hearth against a venging host in arms; facing these rough war-stained men, she forced her trembling body to outward calm and graciousness. Her nerve was not unappreciated. Not one soldier returned his cup without a word of thanks and a look of admiration.

Nor did this pluck go unrewarded. Three months later, passing again through this region as a prisoner, I glimpsed the little cottage still standing in its plot by the flowing river. I want to visit it again after the war. It will always be to me a shrine of the spirit's splendid daring.

Chapter VII
A Duelist from Marburg

A SQUAD OF soldiers stretched out on a bank beckoned me to join them; I did so and at once they begged for news. They were not of an order of super-intelligence, and informed me that it was the French they were to fight at Liége. Unaware that England had entered the lists against Germany, "Belgium" was only a word to them. I took it upon myself to clear up their minds on these points. An officer overheard and plainly showed his disapproval of such missionary activity, yet he could not conceal his own curiosity. I sought to appease him by volunteering some information.

"Japan," I blandly announced, "is about to join the foes of Germany." As the truth, that was unassailable; but as diplomacy it was a wretched fluke.

"You're a fool!" he exploded. "What are you talking about? Japan is one of our best friends, almost as good as America. Those two nations will fight for us - not against us. You're *verrückt*."

That was a severe stricture but in the circumstances I thought best to overlook the reflection upon my mentality. One of the soldiers passed some witticism, evidently at my expense; taking advantage of the outburst of laughter, I made off down the road. They did not offer to detain me. The officer probably reasoned that my being there was guarantee enough of my right to be there, taking it for granted that the regular sentries on the road had passed upon my credentials. However, I made a very strong resolution hereafter to be less zealous in my proclamation of the truth, to hold my tongue and keep walking.

In the midst of my reflections I was startled by a whistle, and, looking back, saw in the distance a puff of steam on what I supposed was the wholly abandoned railway, but there, sure enough, was a train rattling along at a good rate. I could make out soldiers with guns sitting upon the tender, and presumed that they were with these instruments directing the operations of some Belgian engineer and fireman. In a moment more I saw I was mistaken, for at the throttle was a uniformed soldier, and another comrade in his gray-green costume was shoveling coal into the furnace. One of the guards, seeing me plodding on, smilingly beckoned to me to jump aboard. When I took the cue and made a move in that direction he winked his eye and significantly tapped upon the barrel of his gun. The train was loaded with iron rails and timbers, and I speculated as to their use, but farther down the line I saw hundreds of men unloading these, making a great noise as they flung them down the river bank to the water's edge. They were destined for a big pontoon bridge which these men were, with thousands of soldiers, throwing across the stream. Ceaselessly the din and clangor of hammerings rang out over the river.

My way now wound through what was, to all purposes, one German camp, strung for miles along the Meuse. The soldiers were busy with domestic duties. Everywhere there was the cheer and rhythm of well-ordered industry in the open air. In one place thousands of loaves of black bread were being shifted from wagon to wagon. In another they were piling a yard high with mountains of grain. The air was full of the drone of a great mill, humming away at full speed, while the Belgian fields were yielding up their golden harvests to the invaders. Apples in great clusters hung down around the necks of horses tethered in the orchards. With their keepers they were enjoying a respite from their hard fatiguing exertions.

Here and there among the groves, or along the wayside, was a contrivance that looked like a tiny engine; smoke curled out of its chimney and coals blazed brightly in the grate. They were the kitchen-wagons, each making in itself a complete, compact cooking apparatus. Some had immense caldrons with a spoon as large as a spade. In these the stews, put up in dry form and guaranteed to keep for twenty years, were being heated. A savory smell permeated the air and at the sound of the bugle the men clustered about, each looking happy as he received his dish filled with steaming rations.

Through this scene the native Belgians moved freely in and out. Tables had been dragged out into the yard, and around them officers were sitting eating, drinking, and chatting with the peasant women who were serving them and with whom they had set up an *entente cordiale*. Indeed, these Belgians seemed to be rather enjoying this interruption in the monotony of their lives, and a few were making the most of the great adventure. In one case I could not help believing that a certain strikingly-pretty, self-possessed girl was not altogether averse to a war which could thus bring to her side the attentions of such a handsome and gallant set of officers as were gathered round her. At any rate, she was equal to the occasion, and over her little court, which rang with laughter, she presided with a certain rustic dignity and ease.

The ordinary soldier could make himself understood only with motions and sundry gruntings, and consequently had to content himself with smoking in the sun or sleeping in the shade. Everywhere was the atmosphere of physical relaxation after the long journey. So far did my tension wear off, that I even forgot the resolution to hold my tongue. Two officers leaning back in their chairs at a table by the wayside surveyed me intently as I came along. Rather than wait to be challenged, I thought it best to turn aside and ask them my usual question, "How does one get to Liége?"

One of them answered somewhat stiffly, adding, "And where did you learn your German?"

"I was in a German university a few months," I replied.

"Which one?" the officer asked.

"Marburg," I replied.

"Ah!" he said, this time with a smile; "that was mine. I studied philology there."

We talked together of the fine, rich life there, and I spoke of the students' duels I had witnessed a few miles out.

"Ah!" he said, uncovering his head and pointing to the scars across his scalp; "that's where I got these. Perhaps I will get some deeper ones down in this country," he added with a smile.

Ofttimes in the early morning hours I had trudged out to a students' inn on the outskirts of Marburg. As many times I had heard the solemn announcement of the umpire warning all assembled to disperse as the place might be raided by the police and all imprisoned. That was a mere formality. No one left. The umpire forthwith cried *"Los,"* there was a flash of swords in the air as each duelist sought, and sometimes succeeded, in cutting his opponent's face into a Hamburg steak. It was a sanguinary affair and undoubtedly connived at by the officials. When I had asked what was the point of it all, I was told that it developed *Mut* and *Enschlossenheit* - a fine contempt of pain and blood. That dueling was not without its contribution to the general program of German preparedness. Only now the blood-letting was gone at on a colossal scale.

"Yes, that's where I received these cuts," this young officer said, "and if I do not get some too deep down here I'll write to you after the war," he added with another smile. As I gave him my address, I asked for his.

"It's against all the rules," he answered. "It can't be done. But you shall hear from me, I assure you," he said with a hearty handshake.

Only once all the way into Liége did I feel any suspicion directed towards me. That was when I presented my paper to the next guard, a morose-looking individual. He looked at it very puzzled, and put several questions to me. His last one was,

"Where is your home?"

"I come from Boston, Massachusetts," I replied.

Encouraged with my success with the last officers, I ventured to ask him where he came from.

Looking me straight in the eyes, he replied very pointedly, *"Ich komme aus Deutschland."*

Good form among invading armies, I found, precluded the guest making inquiry into any one's antecedents. I made a second resolution to keep my own counsel, as I hurried down the road.

There was no release from his searching eyes until a turn in the highway put an intervening obstacle between myself and him. But this relief was short-lived, for no sooner had I rounded the bend than a cry of "Halt!" shot fear into me. I turned to see a man on a wheel waving wildly at me. I thought it was a summons back to my inquisitor, and the end of my journey. Instead, it was my officer from Marburg, who dismounted, took two letters from his pocket, and asked me if I would have the kindness to deliver them to the *Feld Post* if I got through to Liége. He said that seemed like a God-given opportunity to lift the load off the hearts of his mother and his sweetheart back home. Gladly I took them, with his caution not to drop them into an ordinary letter-box in Liége, but to take them to the *Feld Post* or give them to an officer. I went on my way rejoicing that I could add these letters to my credentials. I now passed down the long street of Jupilles, which was plastered with notices from the German authorities guaranteeing observance of the rights of the citizens of Jupilles, but threatening to visit any overt acts against the soldiers "with the most terrible reprisals."

I arrived on the outskirts of Liége with the expectation of seeing a sorry looking battered city, as the reports which had drifted to the outer world had made it; but considering that it had been the center around which the storm of battle had raged for over two weeks, it showed outwardly but little damage. The chief marks of war were in the shattered windows; the great pontoon bridge of barges, which replaced the dynamited structure by the Rue Leopold, and hundreds of stores and public buildings, flying the white flag with the Red Cross on it. The walls, too, were fairly white with placards posted by order of the German burgomaster Klyper. It was an anachronism to find along the trail of the forty-two centimeter guns warnings of death to persons harboring courier pigeons.

Another bill which was just being posted was the announcement of the war-tax of 50,000,000 francs imposed on the city to pay for the "administration of civil affairs." That was the first of those war-levies which leeched the life blood out of Belgium.

The American consul, Heingartner, threw up his hands in astonishment as I presented myself. No one else had come through since the beginning of hostilities. He begged for newspapers but, unfortunately, I had thrown my lot away, not realizing how completely Liége had been cut off from the outer world. He related the incidents of that first night entry of German troops into Liége. The clatter of machine gun bullets sweeping by the consulate had scarcely ceased when the sounds of gun-butts battering on the doors accompanied by hoarse shouts of *"Auf Steigen"* (get up) reverberated through the street. As the doors unbolted and swung back, officers peremptorily demanded quarters for their troops, receiving with contempt the protests of Heingartner that they were violating precincts under protection of the American flag.

On the following day, however, a whole-hearted apology was tendered along with an invitation to witness the first firing of the big guns.

"Put your fingers in your ears, stand on your toes, and open your mouth," the officer said. There was a terrific concussion, a black speck up in the heavens, and a ton of metal dropped down out of the blue, smashing one of the cupolas of the forts to pieces. That one shot annihilated 260 men. I shuddered as we all do. But it should not be for the sufferings of the killed. For they did not suffer at all. They were wiped out as by the snapping of a finger.

The taking of those 260 bodies out of the world, then, was a painless process. But not so the bringing of these bodies into the world. That cost an infinite sum of pain and anguish. To bring these bodies into being 260 mothers went down into the very Valley of the Shadow of Death. And now in a flash all this life had been sent crashing into eternity. "Women may not bear arms, but they bear men, and so furnish the first munitions of war." Thus are they deeply and directly concerned in the affairs of the state.

The consul with his wife and daughter gave me dinner along with a cordial welcome. At first he was most appreciative of my exploits. Then it seemed to dawn on him that possibly other motives than sheer love of adventure might have spurred me on. The harboring of a possible spy was too large a risk to run in the uncertain temper of the Germans. In that light I took on the aspects of a liability.

The clerks of the two hotels to whom I applied assumed a like attitude.

In fact every one with whom I attempted to hold converse became coldly aloof. Holding the best of intents, I was treated like a pariah. The only one whom I could get a raise from was a book-seller who spoke English. His wrath against the spoilers overcame his discretion, and he launched out into a bitter tirade against them. I reminded him that, as civilians, his fellow-countrymen had undoubtedly been sniping on the German troops. That was too much.

"What would you do if a thief or a murderer entered your house ?" he exploded. "No matter if he had announced his coming, you would shoot him, wouldn't you?"

Realizing that he had confided altogether too much to a casual passerby, he suddenly subsided. The only other comment I could drag out of him was that of a German officer who had told him that "one Belgian could fight as good as four Germans." My request for a lodging-place met with the same evasion from him as from the others.

CHAPTER VIII
THIRTY-SEVEN MILES IN A DAY

"**D**EATH IF YOU try to cross the line after nightfall." Thus my soldier friends picketing the Holland-Belgium frontier had warned me in the morning. That rendezvous with death was not a roseate prospect; but there was something just as ominous about the situation in Liége. To cover the sixteen miles back to the Dutch border before dark was a big task to tackle with blistered feet. I knew the sentries along the way returning, but I knew not the pitfalls for me if I remained in Liége. This drove me to a prompt decision and straightaway I made for the bridge.

It was no prophetically favorable sight that greeted me at the outset. A Belgian, a mere stripling of twenty or thereabouts, had just been shot, and the soldiers, rolling him on a stretcher, were carrying him off. I made so bold as to approach a sentry and ask:

"What has he been doing?"

For an answer the sentry pointed to a nearby notice. In four languages it announced that any one caught near a telegraph pole or wire in any manner that looked suspicious to the authorities would be summarily dealt with. They were carrying him away, poor lad, and the crowd passed on in heedless fashion, as though already grown accustomed to death.

When the troops at the front are taking lives by the thousands, those guarding the lines at the rear catch the contagion of killing. Knowing that this was the temper of some of the sentries, I speeded along at a rapid rate, daring to make one cut across a field, and so came to Jupilles without challenge. Stopping to get a drink there, I realized what a protest my feet were making against the strain to which I was putting them. Luckily, a peasant's vegetable cart was passing, and, jumping on, I was congratulating myself on the relief, when after a few hundred yards the cart turned up a lane, leaving me on the road again with one franc less in my pocket.

There were so few soldiers along this stretch that I drove myself along at a furious pace, slowing up only when I sighted a soldier. I was very hot, and felt my face blazing red as the natives gazed after me stalking so fiercely past them. But the great automobiles plunging by flung up such clouds of dust that my face was being continually covered by this gray powder. What I most feared was lest, growing dizzy, I should lose my head and make incoherent answers.

Faint with the heat I dragged myself into a little wayside place. Everything wore a dingy air of poverty except the gracious keeper of the inn. I pointed to my throat. She understood at once my signs of thirst and quickly produced water and coffee, of which I drank until I was ashamed.

"How much?" I asked.

She shook her head negatively. I pushed a franc or two across the table.

"No," she said smilingly but with resolution. "I can't take it. You need it on your journey. We are all just friends together now."

So my dust and distress had their compensations. They had brought me inclusion in that deeper Belgian community of sorrow.

It was apparent that the Germans were going to make this rich region a great center for their operations and a permanent base of supply. There must have been ten thousand clean-looking cattle on the opposite bank of the river; they were raising a great noise as the soldiers drove their wagons among them, throwing down the hay and grain. Otherwise, the army had settled down from the hustling activities of the morning, and the guards had been posted for the oncoming evening. I knew now that I was progressing at a good pace because near Wandre I noticed a peasant's wagon ahead, and soon overtook it. It was carrying eight or nine Belgian farm-hands, and the horse was making fair time under constant pressure from the driver.

I did not wish to add an extra burden to the overloaded animal, but it was no time for the exercise of sentiment. So I held up a two-franc piece to the driver. He looked at the coin, then he looked at the horse, and then, picking out the meekest and the most inoffensive of his free passengers, he bade him get off and motioned me to take the vacated seat at my right as a first-class paying passenger. Two francs was the fare, and he seemed highly gratified with the sum, little realizing that he could just as well have had two hundred francs for that seat. We stopped once more to hitch on a small woodcart, and with that bumping behind us, we trailed along fearfully slowly. Gladly would I have offered a generous bounty to have him urge his horse along, but I feared to excite suspicion by too lavish an outlay of money. So I sat tight and let my feet dangle off the side, glad of the relief, but feeling them slowly swelling beneath me.

I was saving my head as well as my feet, for the perpetual matching of one's wits in encounters with the guards was continually nerve-frazzling. But now as the cart joggled past, the guard made a casual survey of us all, taking it for granted that I was one of the local inhabitants. For this respite from constant inquisition I was indebted to the dust, grime and sweat that covered me. It blurred out all distinction between myself and the peasants, forming a perfect protective coloration.

To slide past so many guards so easily was a net gain indeed. However, the end of such easy passing came at the edge of Charrate, where the driver turned into his yard, and I was dumped down into an encampment of soldiers. Acting on the militarists' dictum that the best defensive is a strong offensive I pushed my way boldly into the midst of a group gathered round a pump and made signs that I desired a drink. At first they did not understand, or, thinking that I was a native Belgian, they were rather taken aback by such impertinence; but one soldier handed me his cup and another pumped it full. I drank it, and, thanking them, started off. This calm assurance gained me passage past the guard, who had stood by watching the procedure.

In the next six hundred yards I was brought to a standstill by a sudden "Halt!" At one of the posts some soldiers were ringed around a prisoner garbed in the long black regulation cassock of a priest. Though he wore a white handkerchief around his arm as a badge of a peaceful attitude, he was held as a spy. His hands and his eyes were twitching nervously.

He seemed to be glad to welcome the addition of my company into the ranks of the suspects, but he was doomed to disappointment, for I was passed along. The next guard took me to his superior officer directly. But the superior officer was the incarnation of good humor and he was more interested in a little repast that was being made ready for him than in entering into the questions involved in my case.

"Search him for weapons," he said casually, while he himself made a few perfunctory passes over my pockets. No weapons being found, he said, "Let him go. We've done damage here enough."

These interruptions were getting to be distressingly frequent. I had journeyed but a few hundred yards farther when a surly fellow sprang out from behind a wagon and in a raucous voice bade me "Stand by." He had an evil glint in his eye, and was ready to go out of his way hunting trouble. Totally dissatisfied with any answer I could make, he kept roaring louder and louder. There was no doubt that he was venting his spleen upon an unprotected and humble civilian, and that he was thoroughly enjoying seeing me cringe under his bulldozing. It flashed upon me that he might be a self-appointed guardian of the way. So when he began to wax still more arrogant, I simply said, "Take me to your superior officer."

He softened down like a child, and, standing aside, motioned me along.

I would put nothing past a bully of that stripe. He was capable of committing any kind of an atrocity. And his sort undoubtedly did. But what else can one expect from a conscript army, which, as it puts every man on its roster, must necessarily contain the worst as well as the best? Draft 1,000 men out of any community in any country and along with the decent citizens there will be a certain number of cowards, braggarts and brutes. When occasion offers they will rob, rape and murder. To such a vicious strain this fellow belonged.

The soldier whom next I encountered is really typical of the *Gemütlichkeit* of the men who, on the 20th of August, were encamped along the Meuse River. I was moving along fast now under the cover of a hedge which paralleled the road when a voice called out "Halt!" In a step or two I came to a stop. A large fellow climbed over the hedge, and, coming on the road, fell, or rather stumbled over himself, into the ditch. I was afraid he was drunk, and that this tumble would add vexation to his spirits; but he was only tired and over-weighted, carrying a big knapsack and a gun, a number of articles girdled around his waist, along with too much avoirdupois. It seems that even in this conquered territory the Germans never relaxed their vigilance. Fully a thousand men stood guarding the pontoon bridge, and this man, who had gone out foraging and was returning with a bottle of milk, carried his full fighting equipment with him, as did all the others. I gave him a hand and pulled him to his feet, offering to help carry something, as he was breathing heavily; but he refused my aid. As we walked along together I gave him my last stick of chocolate, and, being assured by my demeanor that I was a friend, he showed a real kindly, fatherly interest in me.

"A bunch of robbers, that's what these Belgians are," he asserted stoutly. "They charged me a mark for a quart of milk."

I put my question of the morning to him:

"Is it dangerous traveling along here so late?"

His answer was anything but reassuring.

"Yes, it is very dangerous."

Then he explained that one of his comrades had been shot by a Belgian from the bluffs above that very afternoon and that the men were all very angry. All the Belgians had taken to cover, for the road was totally cleared of pedestrians from this place on to Mouland.

"Well, what am I to do?" I asked.

"Go straight ahead. Swerve neither to the right nor left. Be sure you have no weapons, and stop at once when the guard cries 'Halt!' and you will get through all right. But, above all, be sure to stand stock still immediately at the challenge. Above all - that," he insisted.

"But did I not stop still when you cried 'Halt!' a minute ago!" I asked

"No," he said; "you took two or three steps before you came to a perfect stop. See, this is the way to do it." He started off briskly, and as I cried "Halt!" came to a standstill with marvelous and sudden precision for a man of his weight.

"Do it that way and cry out, 'Ready, here!' and it will be all right."

I would give a great deal for a vignette of that ponderous fellow acting as drillmaster to this stray American. The intensity of the situation rapidly ripened his interest into an affection. I was fretting to get away, but the amenities demanded a more formal leave-taking. At last, however, I broke away, bearing with me his paternal benediction. Far ahead a company of soldiers was forming into line. Just as I reached the place they came to attention, and at a gesture from the captain I walked like a royal personage down past the whole line, feeling hundreds of eyes critically playing upon me. I suspect that the captain had a sense of humor and was enjoying the discomfiture he knew I must feel.

Estimating my advance by the signboards, where distances were marked in kilometers, it appeared that I was getting on with wretched slowness, considering the efforts I was making. At this rate, I knew I should never reach the Holland frontier by nightfall, and from the warnings I had received I dreaded to attempt crossing after sundown. Sleeping in the fields when the whole country was infested by soldiers was out of the question, so I turned to the first open cottage of a peasant and asked him to take me in for the night. He shook his head emphatically, and gave me to understand it would be all his life were worth if he did so. So I rallied my energies for one last effort, and plunged wildly ahead.

The breeze was blowing refreshingly up the river, the road was clear, and soon I was rewarded by seeing the smoke still curling up from the ruins of Visé. I looked at my watch, which pointed to the time for sunset, and yet there was the sun, curiously enough, some distance up from the horizon. The fact of the matter is that I had reset my watch at Liége, and clocks there had all been changed to German time. With a tremendous sense of relief I discovered that I had a full hour more than I had figured on.

There was ample time now to cover the remaining distance, and so I rested a moment before what appeared to be a deserted house. Slowly the shutters were pushed back and a sweet-faced old lady timorously thrust her head out of an upper window. She apparently had been hiding away terror-stricken, and there was something pathetic in the half-trusting way she risked her fate even now. In a low voice she put some question in the local *patois* to me. I could not understand what she was asking, but concluded that she was seeking comfort and assurance. So I sought to convey by much gesturing and benevolent smiling that all was quiet and safe along the Meuse. She may have concluded that I was some harmless, roaming idiot who could not answer a plain question; but it was the best I could do, and I walked on to Visé with the fine feeling of having played the role of comforter.

At Visé I was heartened by two dogs who jumped wildly and joyously around me. I gathered courage enough here to swerve to the right, and from the window of a still burning roadside café extracted three wine-glasses as souvenirs of the trip.

Presently I was in Mouland, whose few forlorn walls grouped about the village church made a pathetic picture as they glowed luminously in the setting sun. A flock of doves were cooing in the blackened ruins. Now I was on the home-stretch; and, that there might be no mistake with my early morning comrades, I cried out in German, "Here comes a friend!" With broad smiles on their faces, they were waiting there to receive me.

They made a not unpicturesque group gathered around their camp-fire. One was plucking a chicken, another making the straw beds for the night. A third was laboriously at work writing a post-card. I ventured the information that I had made over fifty kilometers that day. They punctured my pride somewhat by stating that that was often the regular stint for German soldiers. But, pointing to their own well-made hobnailed boots, they added, "Never in thin rubber soles like yours." After emptying my pockets of eatables and promising to deliver the post-card, I passed once more under the great Dutch banner into neutral territory.

My three Holland friends were there with an automobile, and, greeting me with a hearty *"Gute Knabe!"* whisked me off to Maastricht. For the next three days I did all my writing in bed, nursing a couple of bandaged feet. I wouldn't have missed that trip for ten thousand dollars. I wouldn't go through it again for a hundred thousand.

PART III
WITH THE WAR PHOTOGRAPHERS IN BELGIUM

CHAPTER IX
HOW I WAS SHOT AS A
GERMAN SPY

I N THE LAST days of September, the Belgians moving in and through Ghent in their rainbow-colored costumes, gave to the city a distinctively holiday touch. The clatter of cavalry hoofs and the throb of racing motors rose above the voices of the mobs that surged along the streets.

Service was normal in the cafés. To the accompaniment of music and clinking glasses the dress-suited waiter served me a five-course lunch for two francs. It was uncanny to see this blaze of life while the city sat under the shadow of a grave disaster. At any moment the gray German tide might break out of Brussels and pour its turbid flood of soldiers through these very streets. Even now a Taube hovered in the sky, and from the skirmish-line an occasional ambulance rumbled in with its crimsoned load.

I chanced into Gambrinus' café and was lost in the babbling sea of French and Flemish. Above the melee of sounds, however, I caught a gladdening bit of English. Turning about, I espied a little group of men whose plain clothes stood out in contrast to the colored uniforms of officers and soldiers crowded into the café. Wearied of my efforts at conversing in a foreign tongue, I went over and said:

"Do you really speak English?"

"Well, rather!" answered the one who seemed to act as leader of the group. "We are the only ones now and it will be scarcer still around here in a few days."

"Why?" I asked.

"Because Ghent will be in German hands."

This brought an emphatic denial from one of his confreres who insisted that the Germans had already reached the end of their rope. A certain correspondent, joining in the argument, came in for a deal of banter for taking the war *de luxe* in a good hotel far from the front.

"What do you know about the war?" they twitted him, "You've pumped all your best stories out of the refugees ten miles from the front, after priming them with a glass of beer."

They were a group of young war-photographers to whom danger was a magnet. Though none of them had yet reached the age of thirty, they had seen service in all the stirring events of Europe and even around the globe. Where the clouds lowered and the seas tossed, there they flocked. Like stormy petrels they rushed to the center of the swirling world. That was their element. A free-lance, a representative of the Northcliffe press, and two movie-men comprised this little group and made an island of English amidst the general babel.

Like most men who have seen much of the world, they had ceased to be cynics. When I came to them out of the rain, carrying no other introduction than a dripping overcoat, they welcomed me into their company and whiled away the evening with tales of the Balkan wars.

They were in high spirits over their exploits of the previous day, when the Germans, withdrawing from Melle on the outskirts of the city, had left a long row of cottages still burning. As the enemy troops pulled out the further end of the street, the movie men came in at the other and caught the pictures of the still blazing houses. We went down to view them on the screen. To the gentle throbbing of drums and piano, the citizens of Ghent viewed the unique spectacle of their own suburbs going up in smoke.

At the end of the show they invited me to fill out their automobile on the morrow. Nearly every other motor had been commandeered by the authorities for the "Service Militaire" and bore on the front the letters "S. M." Our car was by no means in the blue-ribbon class. It had a hesitating disposition and the authorities, regarding it as more of a liability than an asset, had passed it over.

But the correspondents counted it a great stroke of fortune to have any car at all; and, that they might continue to have it, they kept it at night carefully locked in a room in the hotel. They had their chauffeur under like supervision. He was one of their kind, and with the cunning of a diplomat obtained the permit to buy petrol, most precious of all treasures in the field of war. Indeed, gasoline, along with courage and discipline, completed the trinity of success in the military mind.

With the British flag flying at the front, we sped away next morning on the road to Termonde. At Melle we came upon the blazing cottages we had seen pictured the night before. Here we encountered a roving band of Belgian soldiers who were in a free and careless mood and evinced a ready willingness to put themselves at our disposal. Under the command of the photographers, they charged across the fields with fixed bayonets, wriggled up through the grass, or, standing behind the trenches, blazed away with their guns at an imaginary enemy. They did some good acting, grim and serious as death. All except one.

This youth couldn't suppress his sense of humor. He could not, or would not, keep from laughing, even when he was supposed to be blowing the head off a Boche. He was properly disciplined and put out of the game, and we went on with our maneuvers to the accompaniment of the clicking cameras until the photographers had gathered in a fine lot of realistic fighting-line pictures.

One of the photographers sat stolidly in the automobile smoking his cigarette while the others were reaping their harvest.

"Why don't you take these too?" I asked.

"Oh," he replied, "I've been sending in so much of that stuff that I just got a telegram from my paper saying, 'Pension off that Belgian regiment which is doing stunts in the trenches.'"

While his little army rested from their maneuvers the Director-in-Chief turned to me and said:

"Wouldn't you like to have a photograph of yourself in these war-surroundings, just to take home as a souvenir?"

That appealed to me. After rejecting some commonplace suggestions, he exclaimed: "I have it. Shot as a German Spy. There's the wall to stand up against; and we'll pick a crack firing-squad out of these Belgians. A little bit of all right, eh?"

I acquiesced in the plan and was led over to the wall while a movie-man whipped out a handkerchief and tied it over my eyes. The director then took the firing squad in hand. He had but recently witnessed the execution of a spy where he had almost burst with a desire to photograph the scene. It had been excruciating torture to restrain himself. But the experience had made him feel conversant with the etiquette of shooting a spy, as it was being done amongst the very best firing-squads. He made it now stand him in good stead.

"Aim right across the bandage," the director coached them. I could hear one of the soldiers laughing excitedly as he was warming up to the rehearsal. It occurred to me that I was reposing a lot of confidence in a stray band of soldiers. Some one of those Belgians, gifted with a lively imagination, might get carried away with the suggestion and act as if I really were a German spy.

"Shoot the blooming blighter in the eye," said one movie man playfully.

"Bally good idea!" exclaimed the other one approvingly, while one eager actor realistically clicked his rifle-hammer. That was altogether too much. I tore the bandage from my eyes, exclaiming:

"It would be a bally good idea to take those cartridges out first." Some fellow might think his cartridge was blank or try to fire wild, just as a joke in order to see me jump. I wasn't going to take any risk and flatly refused to play my part until the cartridges were ejected. Even when the bandage was readjusted "Didn't-know-it-was-loaded" stories still were haunting me. In a moment, however, it was over and I was promised my picture within a fortnight.

A week later I picked up the London *Daily Mirror* from a news-stand. It had the caption:

Belgian Soldiers Shoot a German Spy Caught at Termonde

I opened up the paper and what was my surprise to see a big spread picture of myself, lined up against that row of Melle cottages and being shot for the delectation of the British public. There is the same long raincoat that runs as a *motif* through all the other pictures. Underneath it were the words:

"The Belgians have a short, sharp method of dealing with the Kaiser's rat-hole spies. This one was caught near Termonde and, after being blindfolded, the firing-squad soon put an end to his inglorious career."

One would not call it fame exactly, even though I played the star-rôle. But it is a source of some satisfaction to have helped a royal lot of fellows to a first-class scoop. As the "authentic spy-picture of the war," it has had a broadcast circulation. I have seen it in publications ranging all the way from The Police Gazette to *"Collier's Photographic History of the European War."* In a university club I once chanced upon a group gathered around this identical picture. They were discussing the psychology of this "poor devil" in the moments before he was shot. It was a further source of satisfaction to step in and arbitrarily contradict all their conclusions and, having shown them how totally mistaken they were, proceed to tell them exactly how the victim felt. This high-handed manner nettled one fellow terribly:

"Not so arbitrary, my friend!" he said

"You haven't any right to be so devilish cocksure."

"Haven't I?" I replied. "Who has any better right? I happen to be that identical man!"

But that little episode has been of real value to me. It is said that if one goes through the motions he gets the emotions. I believe that I have an inkling of how a man feels when he momentarily expects a volley of cold lead to turn his skull into a sieve.

That was a very timely picture. It filled a real demand. For spies were at that time looming distressingly large in the public mind. The deeds they had done, or were about to do, cast a cold fear over men by day and haunted them by night. They were in the Allies' councils, infesting the army, planning destruction to the navy. Any wild tale got credence, adding its bit to the general paralysis, and producing a vociferous demand that "something be done." The people were assured that all culprits were being duly sentenced and shot. But there was no proof of it. There were no pictures thereof extant. And that is what the public wanted.

"Give the public what it wants," was the motto of this enterprising newspaper man. Herewith he supplied tangible evidence on which they could feast their eyes and soothe their nerves.

As to the ethics of these pictures, they are "true" in that they are faithful to reality. In this case the photographer acted up to his professional knowledge and staged the pictures as he had actually seen the spy shot. They must find their justification on the same basis as fiction, which is "the art of falsifying facts for the sake of truth." And who would begrudge them the securing of a few pictures with comparative ease?

Most of the pictures which the public casually gazes on have been secured at a price - and a large one, too. The names of these men who go to the front with cameras, rather than with rifles or pens, are generally unknown. They are rarely found beneath the pictures, yet where would be our vivid impression of courage in daring and of skill in doing, of cunning strategy upon the field of battle, of wounded soldiers sacrificing for their comrades, if we had no pictures? A few pictures are faked, but behind most pictures there is another tale of daring and of strategy, and that is the tale concerning the man who took it. That very day thrice these same men risked their lives.

The apparatus loaded in the car, we were off again. Past a few barricades of paving-stones and wagons, past the burned houses which marked the place where the Germans had come within five miles of Ghent, we encountered some uniformed Belgians who looked quite as dismal and dispirited as the fog which hung above the fields. They were the famous Guarde Civique of Belgium. Our Union Jack, flapping in the wind, was very likely quite the most thrilling spectacle they had seen in a week, and they hailed it with a cheer and a cry of *"Vive l'Angleterre!"* (Long live England!) The Guarde Civique had a rather inglorious time of it. Wearisomely in their wearisome-looking uniform, they stood for hours on their guns or marched and counter-marched in dreary patrolling, often doomed not even to scent the battle from afar off.

Whenever we were called to a halt for the examination of our passports, these men crowded around and begged for newspapers. We held up our stock, and they would clamor for the ones with pictures. The English text was unintelligible to most of them, but the pictures they could understand, and they bore them away to enjoy the sight of other soldiers fighting, even if they themselves were denied that excitement. Our question to them was always the same, "Where are the Germans?"

Out of the conflicting reports it was hard to tell whether the Germans were heading this way or not. That they were expected was shown by the sign-posts whose directions had just been obliterated by fresh paint - a rather futile operation, because the Germans had better maps and plans of the region than the Belgians themselves, maps which showed every by-path, well and barn. The chauffeur's brother had been shot in his car by the Germans but a week before, and he didn't relish the idea of thus flaunting the enemy's flag along a road where some German scouting party might appear at any moment. The Union Jack had done good service in getting us easy passage so far, but the driver was not keen for going further with it.

It was proposed to turn the car around and back it down the road, as had been done the previous day. Thus the car would be headed in the home direction, and at sight of the dreaded uniform we could make a quick leap for safety. At this juncture, however, I produced a small Stars and Stripes, which the chauffeur hailed with delight, and we continued our journey now under the aegis of a neutral flag.

It might have secured temporary safety, but only temporary; for if the Englishmen with only British passports had fallen into the hands of the Germans, like their unfortunate kinsmen who did venture too far into the war zone, they too, would have had a chance to cool their ardor in some detention-camp of Germany. This cheerful prospect was in the mind of these men, for, when we espied coming around a distant corner two gray-looking men on horseback, they turned white as the chauffeur cried, "Uhlans!"

It is a question whether the car or our hearts came to a dead standstill first. Our shock was unnecessary. They proved to be Belgians, and assured us that the road was clear all the way to Termonde; and, except for an occasional peasant tilling his fields, the country-side was quite deserted until at Grembergen we came upon an unending procession of refugees streaming down the road. They were all coming out of

Termonde. Termonde, after being taken and retaken, bombarded and burned, was for the moment neutral territory. A Belgian commandant had allowed the refugees that morning to return and gather what they might from among the ruins.

In the early mornings then, they had gone into the city, and now at high noon they were pouring out, a great procession of the dispossessed. They came tracking their way to where - God only knows. All they knew was that in their hearts was set the fear of Uhlans, and in the sky the smoke and flames of their burning homesteads. They came laden with their lares and penates, - mainly dogs, feather beds, and crayon portraits of their ancestors.

Women came carrying on their heads packs which looked like their entire household paraphernalia. The men were more unassuming, and, as a rule, carried a package considerably lighter and comporting more with their superior masculine dignity. I recall one little woman in particular. She was bearing a burden heavy enough to send a strong American athlete staggering down to the ground, while at her side majestically marched her faithful knight, bearing a bird-cage, and there wasn't any bird in it, either.

Nothing could be more mirth-provoking than that sight; yet, strangely enough, the most tear-compelling memory of the war is connected with another bird-cage. Two children rummaging through their ruined home dug it out of the debris. In it was their little pet canary. While fire and smoke rolled through the house it had beat its wings against the bars in vain. Its prison had become its tomb. Its feathers were but slightly singed, yet it was dead with that pathetic finality which attaches itself to only a dead bird - its silver songs and flutterings, once the delight of the children, now stilled forever.

The photographers had long looked for what they termed a first-class sob-picture. Here it was *par excellent*. The larger child stood stroking the feathers of her pet and murmuring over and over "Poor Annette," "Poor Annette!" Then the smaller one snuggling the limp little thing against her neck wept inconsolably.

Instead of seizing their opportunity, the movie man was clearing his throat while the free lance was busy on what he said was a cinder in his eye. Yet this very man had brought back from the Balkan War of 1907 a prime collection of horrors; corpses thrown into the death-cart with arms and legs sticking out like so much stubble; the death-cart creeping away with its ghastly load; and the dumping together of bodies of men and beasts into a pit to be eaten by the lime. This man who had gone through all this with good nerve was now touched to tears by two children crying over their pet canary. There are some things that are too much for the heart of even a war-photographer.

To give the whole exodus the right tragic setting, one is tempted to write that tears were streaming down all the faces of the refugees, but on the contrary, indeed, most of them carried a smile and a pipe, and trudged stolidly along, much as though bound for a fair. Some of our pictures show laughing refugees. That may not be fair, for man is so constituted that the muscles of his face automatically relax to the click of the camera. But as I recall that pitiful procession, there was in it very little outward expression of sorrow.

Undoubtedly there was sadness enough in all their hearts, but people in Europe have learned to live on short rations; they rarely indulge in luxuries like weeping, but bear the most unwonted afflictions as though they were the ordinary fortunes of life. War has set a new standard for grief. So these victims passed along the ready but not before the record of their passing was etched for ever on our moving-picture films. The coming generation will not have to reconstruct the scene from the colored accounts of the journalist, but with their own eyes they can see the hegira of the homeless as it really was.

The resignation of the peasant in the face of the great calamity was a continual source of amazement to us. Zola in *"Le Debacle"* puts into his picture of the battle of Sedan an old peasant plowing on his farm in the valley. While shells go screaming overhead he placidly drives his old white horse through the accustomed furrows. One naturally presumed that this was a dramatic touch of the great novelist. But similar incidents we saw in this Great War over and over again.

We were with Consul van Hee one morning early before the clinging veil of sleep had lifted from our spirits or the mists from the low-lying meadows. Without warning our car shot through a bank of fog into a spectacle of medieval splendor - a veritable Field of the Cloth of Gold, spread out on the green plains of Flanders.

A thousand horses strained at their bridles while their thousand riders in great fur busbies loomed up almost like giants. A thousand pennons stirred in the morning air while the sun burning through the mists glinted on the tips of as many lances. The crack Belgian cavalry divisions had been gathered here just behind the firing-lines in readiness for a sortie; the Lancers in their cherry and green and the Guides in their blue and gold making a blaze of color.

It was as if in a trance we had been carried back to a tourney of ancient chivalry - this was before privations and the new drab uniforms had taken all glamour out of the war. As we gazed upon the glittering spectacle the order from the commander came to us:

"Back, back out of danger!"

"Forward!" was the charge to the Lancers.

The field-guns rumbled into line and each rider unslung his carbine. Putting spurs to the horses, the whole line rode past saluting our Stars and Stripes with a *"Vive L'Amerique."* Bringing up the rear two cassocked priests served to give this pageantry a touch of prophetic grimness.

And yet as the cavalcade swept across the fields thrilling us with its color and its action, the nearby peasants went on spreading fertilizer quite as calm and unconcerned as we were exhilarated.

"Stupid," "Clods," "Souls of oxen," we commented, yet a protagonist of the peasant might point out that it was perhaps as noble and certainly quite as useful to be held by a passion for the soil as to be caught by the glamour of men riding out to slaughter. And Zola puts this in the mind of his peasants.

"Why should I lose a day? Soldiers must fight, but folks must live. It is for me to keep the corn growing."

Deep down into the soil the peasant strikes his roots. Urban people can never comprehend when these roots are cut away how hopelessly lost and adrift this European peasant in particular becomes. Wicked as the Great War has seemed to us in its bearing down upon these innocent folks, yet we can never understand the cruelty that they have suffered in being uprooted from the land and sent forth to become beggars and wanderers upon the highroads of the world.

CHAPTER X
THE LITTLE BELGIAN WHO SAID, "YOU BETCHA"

IN THE FIGHTING around Termonde the bridge over the Scheldt had been three times blown up and three times reconstructed. Wires now led to explosives under the bridge on the Termonde side, and on the side held by the Belgians they led to a table in the room of the commanding officer. In this table was an electric button. By the button stood an officer. The entrance of the Germans on that bridge was the signal for the officer to push that button, and thus to blow both bridge and Germans into bits.

But the Belgians were taking no chances. If by any mishap that electric connection should fail them, it would devolve upon the artillery lined upon the bank to rake the bridge with shrapnel. A roofed-over trench ran along the river like a levee and bristled with machine guns whose muzzles were also trained upon the bridge. Full caissons of ammunition were standing alongside, ready to feed the guns their death-dealing provender, and in the rear, all harnessed, were the horses, ready to bring up more caissons.

Though in the full blaze of day, the gunners were standing or crouching by their guns. The watchers of the night lay stretched out upon the ground, sleeping in the warm sun after their long, anxious vigil. Stumbling in among them, I was pulled back by one of the photographers.

"For heaven's sake," he cried, "don't wake up those men!"

"Why?" I asked.

"Because this picture I'm taking here is to be labeled 'Dead Men in the Termonde Trenches,' and you would have them starting up as though the day of resurrection had arrived."

After taking these pictures we were ready to cross the bridge; but the two sentries posted at this end were not ready to let us. They were very small men, but very determined, and informed us that their instructions were to allow no one to pass over without a permit signed by the General. We produced scores of passes and passports decorated with stamps and seals and covered with myriad signatures. They looked these over and said that our papers were very nice and undoubtedly very numerous, but ungraciously insisted on that pass signed by the General.

So back we flew to the General at Grembergen. I waited outside until my companions emerged from the office waving passes. They were in a gleeful, bantering mood. That evening they apprised me of the fact that all day I had been traveling as a rich American with my private photographers securing pictures for the Belgian Relief Fund.

Leaving our automobile in charge of the chauffeur, we cautiously made our way over the bridge into the city of Termonde, or what was once Termonde, for it is difficult to dignify with the name of city a heap of battered buildings and crumbling brick - an ugly scar upon the landscape.

I was glad to enter the ruins with my companions instead of alone. It was not so much fear of stray bullets from a lurking enemy as the suggestion of the spirits of the slain lingering round these tombs. For Termonde appeared like one vast tomb. As we first entered its sepulchral silences we were greatly relieved that the three specter-like beings who sat huddled up over a distant ruin turned out not to be ghosts, but natives hopelessly and pathetically surveying this wreck that was once called home, trying to rake out of the embers some sort of relic of the past.

A regiment of hungry dogs came prowling up the street, and, remembering the antics of the past week, they looked at us as if speculating what new species of crazy human being we were. To them the world of men must suddenly have gone quite insane, and if there had been an agitator among them he might well have asked his fellow-dogs why they had acknowledged a race of madmen as their masters. Indeed, one could almost detect a sense of surprise that we didn't use the photographic apparatus to commit some new outrage. They stayed with us for a while, but at the sight of our cinema man turning the crank like a machine gun, they turned and ran wildly down the street.

Emptied bottles looted from winecellars were strung along the curbs. To some Germans they had been more fatal than the Belgian bullets, for while one detachment of the German soldiers had been setting the city blazing with petrol from the petrol flasks, others had set their insides on fire with liquors from the wine flasks, and, rolling through the town in drunken orgy, they had fallen headlong into the canal.

There is a relevant item for those who seek further confirmation as to the reality of the atrocities in Belgium. If men could get so drunken and uncontrolled as to commit atrocities on themselves (i.e., self-destruction), it is reasonable to infer that they could commit atrocities on others - and they undoubtedly did. The surprise lies not in the number of such crimes, but the fewness of them.

Three boys who had somehow managed to crawl across the bridge were prodding about in the canals with bamboo poles.

"What are you doing?" we inquired.

"Fishing," they responded.

"What for?" we asked.

"Dead Germans," they replied.

"What do you do with them - bury them?"

"No!" they shouted derisively. "We just strip them of what they've got and shove 'em back in."

Their search for these hapless victims was not motivated by any sentimental reasons, but simply by their business interest as local dealers in helmets, buttons and other German mementos.

We took pictures of these young water-ghouls; a picture of the Hôtel de Ville, the calcined walls standing like a shell, the inside a smoking mass of debris; then a picture of a Belgian mitrailleuse car, manned by a crowd of young and jaunty dare-devils. It came swinging into the square, bringing a lot of bicycles from a German patrol which had just been mowed down outside the city. After taking a shot at an aeroplane buzzing away at a tremendous distance overhead, they were off again on another scouting trip.

I got separated from my party and was making my way alone when a sharp "Hello!" ringing up the street, startled me. I turned to see, not one of the photographers, but a fully-armed, though somewhat diminutive, soldier in Belgian uniform waving his hand at me.

"Hello!" he shouted; "are you an American?"

I could hardly believe my eyes or my ears, but managed to shout back, "Yes, yes, I'm an American. Are you?" I asked dubiously.

"You betcha I'm a 'Merican," he replied, coming quickly up to me. It was my turn again.

"What are you doing down here - fighting?" I put in fatuously.

"What the hell you think I'm doing?" he rejoined.

I now felt quite sure that he was an American. Further offerings of similar "language of small variety but great strength" testified to his sojourn in the States.

"You betcha I'm a 'Merican," he reiterated, "though I was over there but two years. My name is August Ridden. I worked in a lumber-mill in Wagner, Wisconsin. Came back here to visit my family. The war broke out. I was a Reservist and joined my regiment. I'm here on scout-duty. Got to find out when the Germans come back into the city."

"Been in any battles?"

"You betcha," he replied.

"Kill any Germans?"

"You betcha."

"Did you enjoy it?"

"You betcha."

"Any around here now?"

"You betcha. A lot of them down in the bushes over the brook." Then his eyes flashed a sudden fire as though an inspired idea had struck him. "There's no superior officer around," he exclaimed confidentially. "Come right down with me and you can take a pot-shot at the damned Boches with my rifle." He said it with the air of a man offering a rare treat to his best friend. I felt that it devolved on me to exhibit a proper zest for this little shooting-party and save my reputation without risking my skin. So I said eagerly:

"Now are you dead sure that the Germans are down there?" implying that I couldn't afford any time unless the shooting was good.

"You betcha they're down there," was his disconcerting reply. "You can see their green-gray uniforms. I counted sixteen or seventeen of them."

The thought of that sixteen-to-one shot made my cheeks take on the color of the German uniforms. The naked truth was my last resort. It was the only thing that could prevent my zealous friend from dragging me forcibly down to the brookside. He may have heard the chattering of my teeth. At any rate he looked up and exclaimed, "What's the matter? You 'fraid?"

I replied without any hesitation, "You betcha."

The happy arrival of the photographer at this juncture, however, redeemed my fallen reputation; for a soldier is always peculiarly amenable to the charms of the camera and is even willing to quit fighting to get his picture taken. This photograph happens to hit off our little episode exactly. It shows Ridden serene, smiling, confident, and my sort of evasive hangdog look as though, in popular parlance, I had just "got one put over me."

Then, while seated on a battered wall, Ridden poured out his story of the last two months of hardships and horrors. It was the single individual's share in the terrific gruelling that the Belgian army had received while it was beaten back from the eastern frontier to its stand on the river Scheldt. Always being promised aid by the Allies if they would hold out just a little longer, they were led again and again frantically to pit their puny strength against the overwhelming tide out of the North. For the moment they would stay it. Eagerly they would listen for sounds of approaching help, asking every stranger when it was coming. It never came. From position to position they fell back, stubbornly fighting, a flaming pillar of sparks and clouds of smoke marking the path of their retreat.

Though smashed and broken that army was never crushed. Its spirit was incarnate in this cheerful and undaunted Ridden. He recounted his privations as nonchalantly as if it was just the way that he had planned to spend his holiday. As a farewell token he presented me with an epaulet from an officer he had killed, and a pin from a German woman spy he had captured.

"Be sure to visit me when you get back to America," I cried out down the street to him.

He stood waving his hand in farewell as in greeting, the same happy ingenuous look upon his face and sending after me in reply the same old confident standby, "You betcha." But I do not cherish a great hope of ever seeing Ridden again. The chances are that, like most of the Belgian army, he is no longer treading the gray streets of those demolished cities, but whatever golden streets there may be in the City Celestial. War is race suicide. It kills the best and leaves behind the undermuscled and the under-brained to propagate the species.

Striking farther into the heart of the ruins, we beheld in a section all burned and shattered to the ground a building which stood straight up like a cliff intact and undamaged amidst the general wreckage. As we stumbled over the debris, imagine our surprise when an old lady of about seventy thrust her head out of a basement window. She was the owner of the house, and while the city had been the fighting ground for the armies she had, through it all, bravely stuck to her home.

"I was born here, I have always lived here, and I am going to die here," she said, with a look of pride upon her kindly face.

Madame Callebaut-Ringoot was her name. During the bombardment of the town she had retired to the cellar; but when the Germans entered to burn the city she stood there at the door watching the flames rolling up from the warehouses and factories in the distance. Nearer and nearer came the billowing tide of fire. A fountain of sparks shooting up from a house a few hundred yards away marked the advance of the firing squad into her street, but she never wavered. Down the street came the spoilers, relentless, ruthless, and remorseless, sparing nothing. They came like priests of the nether world, anointing each house with oil from the petrol flasks and with a firebrand dedicating it to the flames. Everyone, panic-stricken, fled before them. Every one but this old lady, who stood there bidding defiance to all the Kaiser's horses and all the Kaiser's men.

"I saw them smashing in the door of the house across the way," said Madame Callebaut, "and when the flames burst forth they rushed over here, and I fell down on my knees before them, crying out, 'For the love of Heaven, spare an old woman's house!'"

It must have been a dramatic, soul-curdling sight, with the wail of the woman rising above the crashing walls and the roaring flames. And it must have been effective pleading to stop men in their wild rush lusting to destroy. But Madame Callebaut was endowed with powerful emotions. Carried away in her recital of the events, she fell down on her knees before me, wringing her hands and pleading so piteously that I felt for a moment as if I were a fiendish Teuton with a firebrand about to set the old lady's house afire. I can understand how the wildest men capitulated to such pleadings, and how they came down the steps to write, in big, clear words,

"NICHT ANBRENNEN"
(Do not set fire to)

Only they unwittingly wrote it upon her neighbor's walls, thus saving both houses.

How much a savior of other homes Madame Callebaut had been Termonde will never know. Certainly she made the firing squad first pause in the wild debauch of destruction. For frequently now an undamaged house stood with the words chalked on its front, "Only harmless old woman lives here; do not burn down." Underneath were the numbers and initials of the particular corps of the Kaiser's Imperial Army. Often the flames had committed *lèse majesté* by leaping onto the forbidden house, and there amidst the charred ruins stood a door or a wall bearing the mocking inscription, *"Nicht Anbrennen."*

Another house, belonging to Madame Louise Bal, bore the words, "Protected; *Gute alte Leute hier*" (good old people here). A great shell from a distant battery had totally disregarded this sign and had torn through the parlor, exploding in the back yard, ripping the clothes from the line, but touching neither of the inmates. As the Chinese ambassador pertinently remarked when reassured by Whitlock that the Germans would not bombard the embassies, "Ah! but a cannon has no eyes."

These houses stood up like lone survivors above the wreckage wrought by fire and shell, and by contrast served to emphasize the dismal havoc everywhere. "So this was once a city," one mused to himself; "and these streets, now sounding with the footfalls of some returning sentry, did they once echo with the roar of traffic? And those demolished shops, were they once filled with the babble of the traders? Over yonder in that structure, which looks so much like a church, did the faithful once come to pray and to worship God? Can it be that these courtyards, now held in the thrall of death-like silence, once rang to the laughter of the little children?" One said to himself, "Surely this is some wild dream. Wake up."

But hardly a dream, for here were the ruins of a real city, and fresh ruins too. Still curling up from the church was smoke from the burning rafters, and over there the hungry dogs, and the stragglers mournfully digging something out of the ruins. However preposterous it seemed, none the less it was a city that yesterday ran high with the tide of human life. And thousands of people, when they recall the lights and shadows, the pains and raptures, which make up the thing we call life, will think of Termonde. Thousands of people, when they think of home and all the tender memories that cluster round that word, say "Termonde." And now where Termonde was there is a big black ragged spot - an ugly gaping wound in the landscape. There are a score of other wounds like that.

There are thousands of them.

There is one bleeding in every Belgian heart.

The sight of their desolated cities cut the soldiers to the quick.

They turned the names of those cities into battle cries. Shouting "Remember Termonde and Louvain," these Belgians sprang from the trenches and like wild men flung themselves upon the foe.

CHAPTER XI
ATROCITIES AND THE SOCIALIST

"WITH THESE SENTRIES holding us up at every cross-roads, there is no use trying to get to Antwerp," said the free-lance.

"Yes, there is," retorted the chauffeur.

"Watch me the next time." He beckoned to the first sentry barring the way, and, leaning over, whispered into the man's ear a single word. The sentry saluted, and, stepping to one side, motioned us on in a manner almost deferential. We had hardly been compelled to stop.

After our tedious delays this was quite exhilarating. How our chauffeur obtained the password we did not know, nor did we challenge the inclusion of 8 francs extra in his memorandum of expenses. As indicated, he was a man of parts. The magic word of the day, "France," now opened every gate to us.

Behind the Antwerp fortifications the Belgian sappers and miners were on an organized rampage of destruction. On a wide zone every house, windmill and church was either going up in flames or being hammered level to the ground.

We came along as the oil was applied to an old house and saw the flames go crackling up through the rafters. The black smoke curled away across the wasted land and the fire glowed upon the stolid faces of the soldiers and the trembling woman who owned it. To her it was a funeral pyre. Her home endeared by lifetime memories was being offered up on the altar of Liberty and Independence. Starting with the invaders on the western frontier, clear through to Antwerp by the sea, a wild black swathe had been burnt.

By such drastic methods space was cleared for the guns in the Belgian forts, and to the advancing besiegers no protection would be offered from the raking fire. The heart of a steel-stock owner would have rejoiced to see the maze of wire entanglement that ran everywhere. In one place a tomato-field had been wired; the green vines, laden with their rich red fruit, were intertwined with the steel vines bearing their vicious blood-drawing barbs whose intent was to make the red field redder still. We had just passed a gang digging man-holes and spitting them with stakes, when an officer cried:

"Stop! No further passage here. You must turn back."

"Why?" we asked protestingly.

"The entire road is being mined," he replied.

Even as he spoke we could see a liquid explosive being poured into a sort of cup, and electric wires connected. The officer pictured to us a regiment of soldiers advancing, with the full tide of life running in their veins, laughing and singing as they marched in the smiling sun. Suddenly the road rocks and hell heaves up beneath their feet; bodies are blown into the air and rained back to the earth in tiny fragments of human flesh; while brains are spattered over the ground, and every crevice runs a rivulet of blood. He sketched this in excellent English, adding:

"A magnificent climax for Christian civilization, eh! And that's my business. But what else can one do?"

For the task of setting this colossal stage for death, the entire peasant population had been mobilized to assist the soldiers. In self-defense Belgium was thus obliged to drive the dagger deep into her own bosom. It seemed indeed as if she suffered as much at her own hands, as at the hands of the enemy. To arrest the advancing scourge she impressed into her service dynamite, fire and flood. I saw the sluice-gates lifted and meadows which had been waving with the golden grain of autumn now turned into silver lakes. So suddenly had the waters covered the land that hay-cocks bobbed upon the top of the flood, and peasants went out in boats to dredge for the beets and turnips which lay beneath the waters.

The roads were inundated and so we ran along an embankment

which, like a levee, lifted itself above the water wastes. The sun, sinking down behind the flaming poplars in the west, was touching the rippling surface into myriad colors. It was like a trip through Fairyland, or it would have been, were not men on all sides busy preparing for the bloody shambles.

After these elaborate defensive works the Belgians laughed at any one taking Antwerp, the impregnable fortress of Western Europe. The Germans laughed, too. But it was the bass, hollow laugh of their great guns placed ten to twenty miles away, and pouring into the city such a hurricane of shell and shrapnel that they forced its evacuation by the British and the Belgians. Through this vast array of works which the reception committee had designed for their slaughter, the Germans came marching in as if on dress parade.

A few shells were even now crashing through Malines and had played havoc with the carillon in the cathedral tower. During a lull in the bombardment we climbed a stairway of the belfry where, above us, balanced great stones which a slight jar would send tumbling down. On and up we passed vents and jagged holes which had been ripped through these massive walls as if they were made of paper. It was enough to carry the weight of one's somber reflections without the addition of cheerful queries of the movie-man as to "how would you feel if the German gunners suddenly turned loose again?"

We gathered in a deal of stone ornaments that had been shot down and struggled with a load of them to our car. Later they became a weight upon our conscience. When Cardinal Mercier starts the rebuilding of his cathedral, we might surprise him with the return of a considerable portion thereof. To fetch these souvenirs through to England, we were compelled to resort to all the tricks of a gang of smugglers.

I made also a first rate collection of German posters. By day I observed the location of these placards, announcing certain death to those who "sniped on German troops," "harbored courier-pigeons," or "destroyed" these self-same posters.

At night with trembling hands I laid cold compresses on them until the adhering paste gave way; then, tucking the wet sheets beneath my coat, I stole back to safety. At last in England I feasted my eyes on the precious documents, dreaming of the time when posterity should rejoice in the possession of these posters relating to the German overlordship of Belgium, and give thanks to the courage of their collector. Unfortunately, their stained and torn appearance grated on the aesthetic sensibilities of the maid.

"Where are they?" I demanded on my return to my room one time, as I missed them.

"Those nasty papers?" she inquired naïvely.

"Those priceless souvenirs," I returned severely. She did not comprehend, but with a most aggravatingly sweet expression said:

"They were so dirty, sir, I burned them all up."

She couldn't understand why I rewarded her with something akin to a fit of apoplexy, instead of a liberal tip. That day was a red-letter one for our photographers. They paid the price in the risks which constantly strained their nerves. But in it they garnered vastly more than in the fortnight they had hugged safety.

But, despite all our efforts, there was one object that we were after that we never did attain. That was a first-class atrocity picture. There were atrocity stories in endless variety, but not one that the camera could authenticate. People were growing chary of verbal assurances of these horrors; they yearned for some photographic proof, and we yearned to furnish it.

"What features are you looking for?" was the question invariably put to us on discovering our cameras.

"Children with their hands cut off," we replied. "Are there any around here?"

"Oh, yes! Hundreds of them," was the invariable assurance.

"Yes, but all we want is one - just one in flesh and bone. Where can we find that?"

The answer was ever the same. "In the hospital at the rear, or at the front." "Back in such-and-such a village," etc. Always somewhere else; never where we were.

Let no one attempt to gloss the cruelties perpetrated in Belgium. My individual wish is to see them pictured as crimson as possible, that men may the fiercer revolt against the shame and horror of this red butchery called war. But this is a record of just one observer's reactions and experiences in the war zone. After weeks in this contested ground, the word "atrocity" now calls up to my mind hardly anything I saw in Belgium, but always the savageries I have witnessed at home in America.

For example, the organized frightfulness that I once witnessed in Boston. Around the strikers picketing a factory were the police in full force and a gang of thugs. Suddenly at the signal of a shrill whistle, sticks were drawn from under coats and, right and left, men were felled to the cobblestones. After a running fight a score were stretched out unconscious, upon the square. As blood poured out of the gashes, like tigers intoxicated by the sight and smell thereof, the assailants became frenzied, kicking and beating their victims, already insensible. In a trice the beasts within had been unleashed.

If in normal times men can lay aside every semblance of restraint and decency and turn into raging fiends, how much greater cause is there for such a transformation to be wrought under the stress of war when, by government decree, the sixth commandment is suspended and killing has become glorified. At any rate my experiences in America make credible the tales told in Belgium.

But there are no pictures of these outrages such as the Germans secured after the Russian drive into their country early in the war. Here are windrows of mutilated Germans with gouged eyes and mangled limbs, attesting to that same senseless bestial ferocity which lies beneath the veneer.

All the photographers were fired with desire to make a similar picture in Belgium, yet though we raced here and there, and everywhere that rumor led us, we found it but a futile chase.

Through the Great Hall in Ghent there poured 100,000 refugees. Here we pleaded how absolutely imperative it was that we should obtain an atrocity picture. The daughter of the burgomaster, who was in charge, understood our plight and promised to do her best. But out of the vast concourse she was able to uncover but one case that could possibly do service as an atrocity.

It was that of a blind peasant woman with her six children. The photographers told her to smile, but she didn't, nor did the older children; they had suffered too horribly to make smiling easy. When the Germans entered the village the mother was in bed with her day-old baby. Her husband was seized and, with the other men, marched away, as the practice was at that period of the invasion, for some unaccountable reason. With the roof blazing over her head, she was compelled to arise from her bed and drag herself for miles before she found a refuge. I related this to a German later and he said: "Oh, well, there are plenty of peasant women in the Fatherland who are hard at work in the fields three days after the birth of their child."

The Hall filled with women wailing for children, furnished heartrending sights, but no victim bore such physical marks as the most vivid imagination could construe into an atrocity.

"I can't explain why we don't get a picture," said the free lance. "Enough deviltry has been done. I can't see why some of the stuff doesn't come through to us."

"Simply because the Germans are not fools," replied the movie-man; "when they mutilate a victim, they go through with it to the finish. They take care not to let telltales go straggling out to damn them."

Some one proposed that the only way to get a first-class atrocity picture was to fake it. It was a big temptation, and a fine field for the exercise of their inventive genius. But on this issue the chorus of dissent was most emphatic.

The nearest that I came to an atrocity was when in a car with Van Hee, the American vice-consul at Ghent. Van Hee was a man of laconic speech and direct action. I told him what Lethbridge, the British consul, had told me; viz., that the citizens of Ghent must forthwith erect a statue of Van Hee in gold to commemorate his priceless services. "The gold idea appeals to me, all right," said Van Hee, "but why put it in a statue?" He routed me out at five one morning to tell me that I could go through the German lines with Mr. Fletcher into Brussels. We left the

Belgian Army cheering the Stars and Stripes, and came to the outpost of sharpshooters. Crouching behind a barricade, they were looking down the road. They didn't know whether the Germans were half a mile, two miles, or five miles down that road.

Into that uncertain No-Man's-Land we drove with only our honking to disturb the silence, while our minds kept growing specters of Uhlans the size of Goliath. Fletcher and I kept up a hectic conversation upon the flora and fauna of the country. But Van Hee, being of strong nerves, always gleefully brought the talk back to Uhlans.

"How can you tell an Uhlan?" I faltered.

"If you see a big gray man on horseback, with a long lance, spearing children," said Van Hee, "why, that's an Uhlan."

Turning a sharp corner, we ran straight ahead into a Belgian bicycle division - scouting in this uncertain zone. In a flash they were off their wheels, rifles at their shoulders and fingers on triggers.

Two boys, gasping with fear, thrust their guns up into our very faces. In our gray coats we had been taken for a party of German officers. They were positive that a peasant was hanging in a barn not far away. But we insisted that our nerves had had enough for the day. Even Van Hee was willing to let the conversation drift back to flowers and birds. We drove along in chastened spirit until hailed by the German outpost, about five miles from where we had left the Belgians. No-Man's-Land was wide in those days.

But what is it that really constitutes an atrocity? In a refugee shed, sleeping on the straw, we found an old woman of 88. All that was left to her was her shawl, her dress, and the faint hope of seeing two sons for whom she wept. Extreme old age is pitiful in itself. With homelessness it is tragic. But such homeless old age as this, with scarce one flickering ray of hope, is double-distilled tragedy. If some marauder had bayoneted her, and she had died therefrom, it would have been a kindly release from all the anguish that the future now held in store for her. Of course that merciful act would have constituted an atrocity, because it would have been a breach in the rules of the war game.

But in focusing our attention upon the violations of the code, we are apt to forget the greater atrocity of the violation of Belgium, and the whole hideous atrocity of the great war. That is getting things out of proportion, for the sufferings entailed by these technical atrocities are infinitesimal alongside of those resulting from the war itself.

Another point has been quite overlooked. In recounting the atrocities wrought by Prussian Imperialism, no mention is made of those that it has committed upon its own people. And yet at any rate a few Germans suffered in the claws of the German eagle quite as cruelly as any Belgians did. One fine morning in September three Germans came careening into Ghent in a great motor car. They were dazed to find no evidence of their army which they supposed was in possession. Before the men became aware of their mistake, a Belgian mitrailleuse poured a stream of lead into their midst, killing two of them outright. The third German, with a ball in his neck, was rescued by Van Hee and placed under the protection of the American flag.

Incidentally that summary action, followed by a quick visit to the German general in his camp on the outskirts, saved the city. That is a long story. It is told in Alexander Powell's *"Fighting in Flanders,"* but it suffices here to state that by a pact between the Belgian burgomaster of Ghent and the German commandant it was understood that the wounded man was not to be considered a prisoner, but under the jurisdiction of the American Consulate.

A week after this incident Van Hee paid his first visit to this wounded man in the Belgian hospital. He was an honest fellow of about forty - the type of working-man who had aspired to nothing beyond a chance to toil and raise a family for the Fatherland. *Weltpolitik*, with its vaunting boast of "World-power or Downfall," was meaningless to him and his comrades gathered in the beer-gardens on a Sunday.

Suddenly out of this quiet, uneventful life he was called to the colors and sent killing and burning through the Belgian villages. His officers had told him that it would be a sorry thing for any German soldier to be captured, for these Belgians, maddened by the pillage of their country, would take a terrible revenge upon any luckless wretches that fell into their hands. Now, more suddenly than anything else had ever happened in his life, a bullet had stabbed him in the throat and he found himself a prisoner at the mercy of these dreaded Belgians.

"Why are they tending me so carefully during these last seven days?" "Are they getting me ready for the torturing?" "Are they making me well in order that I may suffer all the more?" Grim speculation of that kind must have been running through his simple mind. For when we opened the door of his room, he slunk cowering over to his bed, staring at us as if we were inquisitors about to lead him away to the torture chamber, there to suffer vicariously for all the crimes of the German army. His body, already shrunken by overwork, visibly quivered before us, the perspiration beading on his ashen face.

We had come to apprise him of his present status as a citizen under the protectorate of America.

Van Hee approached the subject casually with the remark: "You see, you are not a Frenchman!"

"No, I am not a Frenchman," the quailing fellow mechanically repeated.

"And you are not a Belgian," resumed Van Hee.

He was not quite sure about disclaiming that, but he saw what was expected of him. So he faltered: "No, I am not a Belgian."

"And you are not an Englishman, eh?"

According to formula he answered:

"No, I am not an Englishman!" but I sensed a bit more of emphasis in the disavowal of any English taint to his blood.

Van Hee was taking this process of elimination in order to clear the field so that his man could grasp the fact that he was to all intents an American, and at last he said:

"No longer are you a German either."

The poor fellow was in deep seas, and breathing hard. Everything about him proclaimed the fact that he was a German, even to his field-gray uniform, and he knew it. But he did not venture to contradict Van Hee, and he whispered hoarsely: "No, I am not a German either."

He was completely demoralized, a picture of utter desolation.

"If you are not German, or Belgian, or French, or English, what are you then?"

The poor fellow whimpered: "*O Gott!* I don't know what I am."

"I'll tell you what you are. You're an American!" exclaimed Van Hee with great gusto. "That's what you are - an American! Get that? An American!"

"*Ja, ja ich bin ein Amerikaner!*" he eagerly cried ("Yes, yes, I am an American!"), relieved to find himself no longer a man without a country. Had he been told that he was a Hindoo, or an Eskimo, he would have acquiesced as obediently.

But when he was shown an American flag and it began to dawn on him that he had nothing more to fear from his captors, his tenseness relaxed. And when Van Hee said: "As the American consul I shall do what I can for you. What is it you want the most?" a light shone in the German's eyes and he replied:

"I want to go home. I want to see my wife and children."

"I thought you came down here because you wanted to see the war," said Van Hee.

"War!" he gasped, and putting hands up to his eyes as if to shut out some awful sights, he began muttering incoherently about "Louvain," "children screaming," "blood all over his breast," repeating constantly *"schrecklich, schrecklich."* "I don't want to see any more war. I want to see my wife and my three children!"

"The big guns! Do you hear them?" I said.

"I don't want to hear them," he answered, shaking his head.

"They're killing you Germans by the thousands down there," announced Van Hee. "I should think you would want to get out and kill the French and the English."

"I don't want to kill anybody," he repeated. "I never did want to kill anybody. I only want to go home." As we left him he was repeating a refrain: "I want to go home" - *"Schrecklich, schrecklich."* "I never did want to kill anybody."

Every instinct in that man's soul was against the murder he had been set to do. His conscience had been crucified. A ruthless power had invaded his domain, dragged him from his hearthside, placed a gun in his hands and said to him: "Kill!"

Perhaps before the war, as he had drilled along the German roads, he had made some feeble protest. But then war seemed so unreal and so far away; now the horror of it was in his soul.

A few days later Van Hee was obliged to return him to the German lines. Again he was marched out to the shambles to take up the killings against which his whole nature was in rebellion. No slave ever went whipped to his task with greater loathing.

Once I saw slowly plodding back into Brussels a long gray line of soldiers; the sky, too, was gray and a gray weariness had settled down upon the spirits of these troops returning from the destruction of a village. I was standing by the roadside holding in my arms a refugee baby.

Its attention was caught by an officer on horseback and in baby fashion it began waving its hand at him. Arrested by this sudden gleam of human sunshine the stern features of the officer relaxed into a smile. Forgetting for the moment his dignity he waved his hand at the baby in a return salute, turning his face away from his men that they might not see the tears in his eyes. But we could see them.

Perhaps through those tears he saw the mirage of his own fireside. Perhaps for the moment his homing spirit rested there, and it was only the body from which the soul had fled that was in the saddle here before us riding through a hostile land. Perhaps more powerfully than the fulminations of any orator had this greeting of a little child operated to smite him with the senseless folly of this war. Who knows but that right then there came flashing into his mind the thought: "Why not be done with this cruel orphaning of Belgian babies, this burning down of their homes and turning them adrift upon the world?"

Brutalizing as may be the effect of militarism in action, fortified as its devotees may be by all the iron ethics of its code, I cannot help but believe that here again the ever-recurring miracle of repentance and regeneration had been wrought by the grace of a baby's smile; that again this stern-visaged officer had become just a human being longing for peace and home, revolting against laying waste the peace and homes of his fellowmen. But to what avail? All things would conspire to make him conform and stifle the revolt within. How could he escape from the toils in which he was held? Next morrow or next week he would again be in the saddle riding out to destruction.

The irony of history again! It was this German folk who said, centuries ago: "No religious authority shall invade the sacred precincts of the soul and compel men to act counter to their deepest convictions." In a costly struggle the fetters of the church were broken. But now a new iron despotism is riveted upon them. The great state has become the keeper of men's consciences. The dragooning of the soul goes on just the same. Only the power to do it has been transferred from the priests to the officers of the state. To compel men to kill when their whole beings cry out against it, is an atrocity upon the souls of men as real as any committed upon the bodies of the Belgians.

Amidst the wild exploits and wilder rumors of those crucial days when Belgium was the central figure in the world-war, the calmness of the natives was a source of constant wonder. In the regions where the Germans had not yet come they went on with their accustomed round of eating, drinking and trading with a *sang froid* that was distressing to the fevered outsider.

Yet beneath this surface calmness and gayety ran a smoldering hate, of whose presence one never dreamed, unless he saw it shoot out in an ugly flare.

I saw this at Antwerp when about 300 of us had been herded into one of the great halls. As one by one the suspects came up to the exit gate to be overhauled by the examiners, I thought that there never could be such a complacent, dead-souled crowd as this. They had dully waited for two hours with scarce a murmur.

The most pathetic weather-worn old man - a farm drudge, I surmise - came up to the exit. All I heard were the words of the officer: "You speak German, eh?"

At a flash this dead throng became an infuriated blood-thirsting mob. *"Allemand! Espion!"* it shouted, swinging forward until the gates sagged. "Kill him! Kill the damned German!"

The mob would have put its own demand into execution but for the soldiers, who flung the poor quivering fellow into one corner and pushed back the Belgians, eager to trample him to the station floor.

There was the girl Yvonne, who, while the color was mounting to her pretty face, informed us that she "wanted the soldiers to *keel* every German in the world. No," she added, her dark eyes snapping fire, "I want them to leave just one. The last one I shall *keel* myself!"

Yet, every example of Belgian ferocity towards the spoilers one could match with ten of Belgian magnanimity. We obtained a picture of Max Crepin, *carbinier voluntaire*, in which he looks seventy years of age - he was really seventeen. At the battle of Melle be had fallen into the hands of the Germans after a bullet had passed clean through both cheeks. In their retreat the Germans had left Max in the bushes, and he was now safe with his friends.

He could not speak, but the first thing he wrote in the little book the nurse handed him was, "The Germans were very kind to me." There was a line about his father and mother; then "We had to lie flat in the bushes for two days. One German took off his coat and wrapped it around me, though he was cold himself. Another German gave me all the water in his canteen." Then came a line about a friend, and finally: "The Germans were very kind to me." I fear that Max would not rank high among the haters.

Whenever passion swept and tempted to join their ranks, the figure of Gremberg comes looming up to rebuke me. He was a common soldier whose *camaraderie* I enjoyed for ten days during the skirmishing before Antwerp. In him the whole tragedy of Belgium was incarnated. He had lost his two brothers; they had gone down before the German bullets. He had lost his home; it had gone up in flames from the German torch. He had lost his country; it had been submerged beneath the gray horde out of the north.

"Why is it, Gremberg," I asked, "you never rage against the Boches? I should think you would delight to lay your hands on every German and tear him into bits. Yet you don't seem to feel that way."

"No, I don't," he answered. "For if I had been born a Boche, I know that I would act just like any Boche. I would do just as I was ordered to do."

"But the men who do the ordering, the officers and the military caste, the whole Prussian outfit?"

"Well, I have it in for that crowd," Gremberg replied, "but, you see, I'm a Socialist, and I know they can't help it. They get their orders from the capitalists."

The capitalists, he explained, were likewise caught in the vicious toils of the system and could act no differently. Bayonet in hand, he expounded the whole Marxian philosophy as he had learned it at the Voorhuit in Ghent. The capitalists of Germany were racing with the capitalists of England for the markets of the world, so they couldn't help being pitted against each other. The war was simply the transference of the conflict from the industrial to the military plane, and Belgium, the ancient cockpit of Europe, was again the battlefield.

He emphasized each point by poking me with his bayonet. As an instrument of argument it is most persuasive. When I was a bit dense, he would press harder until I saw the light. Then he would pass on to the next point.

I told him that I had been to *Humanité's* office in Paris after Jaurès was shot, and the editors, pointing to a great pile of anti-war posters, explained that so quickly had the mobilization been accomplished, that there had been no time to affix these to the walls.

"The French Socialists had some excuse for their going out to murder their fellow workers," I said, "and the Germans had to go or get shot, but you are a volunteer. You went to war of your own free-will, and you call yourself a Socialist."

"I am, but so am I a Belgian!" he answered hotly. "We talked against war, but when war came and my land was trampled, something rose up within me and made me fight. That's all. It's all right to stand apart, but you don't know."

I did know what it was to be passion swept, but, however, I went on baiting him.

"Well, I suppose that you are pretty well cured of your Socialism, because it failed, like everything else."

"Yes, it did," he answered regretfully, "but at any rate people are surprised at Socialists killing one another - not at the Christians. And anyhow if there had been twice as many priests and churches and lawyers and high officials, that would not have delayed the war. It would have come sooner; but if there had been twice as many Socialists there would have been no war."

The free-lance interrupted to call him out for a picture before it was too dark. Gremberg took his position on the trench, his hand shading his eyes. It is the famous iron trench at Melle from which the Germans had withdrawn. He is not looking for the enemy. If they were near, ten bullets would have brought him down in as many seconds. He is looking into the West.

And to me he is a symbol of all the soldiers of Europe, and all the women of Europe who huddle to their breasts their white-faced, sobbing children. They are all looking into the West, for there lies Hope. There lies America. And their prayer is that the young republic of the West shall not follow the blood-rusted paths of militarism, but somehow may blaze the way out of chaos into a new world-order.

PART IV
LOVE AMONG THE RUINS

Chapter XII
The Beating of
"The General"

"THE SADDEST SOUND in all the world," says Sardou, "is the beating of 'the General.'" On that fateful Saturday afternoon in August, after nearly fifty years of silence through the length and breadth of France, there sounded again the ominous throbbing of the drums calling for the general mobilization of the nation. At its sound the French industrial army melted into a military one. Ploughshares and pruning-hooks were beaten into machine-guns and Lebel rifles. The civilian straightway became a soldier.

We were returning from Malmaison, the home where Napoleon spent with Josephine the happiest moments of his life. Our Parisian guide and chauffeur were in chatting, cheerful mood though fully alive to all the rumors of war. They were sons of France, from their infancy drilled in the idea that some day with their comrades they were to hear this very drum calling them to march from their homes; they had even been taught to cherish the coming of this day when they should redeem the tarnished glory of France by helping to plant the tricolor over the lost provinces of Alsace and Lorraine.

But that the dreaded, yet hoped-for day had really arrived, seemed preposterous and incredible - incredible until we drove into the village of Reuilly where an eager crowd, gathering around a soldier with a drum, caused our chauffeur to draw sharply up beside the curb and we came to a stop twenty feet from the drummer. He was a man gray enough to have been, if not a soldier, at least a drummer boy in 1870. The pride that was his now in being the official herald of portentous news was overcast by an evident sorrow.

As if conscious of the fact that he was to pound not on the dead dry skin of his drum, but on living human hearts, he hesitated a moment before he let the sticks falls. Then sharp and loud throbbed the drum through the still-hushed street. Clear and resolute was the voice in which he read the order for mobilization. The whole affair took little more than a minute. Those who know how heavily the disgrace and disaster of 1870 lie upon the French heart will admit that it is fair to say that all their life this crowd had lived for this moment. Now that it had come, they took it with tense white looks upon their faces. But not a cheer, not a cry, not a shaking of the fist.

The only outwardly tragic touch came from our chauffeur. When he heard the words *"la mobilization"* he flung down his cap, threw up his hands, bowed his head a second, then gripped his steering wheel and, for fifteen miles, drove desperately, accurately, as though his car were a winged bullet shooting straight into the face of the enemy. That fifteen-mile run from Reuilly to Paris was through a long lane of sorrow: for not to one section or class, but to *all* France had come the call to mobilize. Every home had been summoned to the sacrifice of its sons.

We witnessed nowhere any wailings or wringing of hands or frantic, foolish pleading to stay at home. Long ago the question of their dear ones going had been settled. Through the years they had made ready their hearts for this offering and now they gave with a glad exaltation. How bravely the French woman met the demand upon her, only those of us who moved in and out among the homes during those days of mobilization can testify. The "General" was indeed to these mothers, wives and sweethearts left behind the saddest sound in all the world.

But if it were so sad as Sardou said in 1870, when 500,000 answered to its call, how infinitely sadder was it in 1914 when ten times that number responded to its wild alarum, a million never returning to the women that had loved them. But such statistics are just the unemotional symbols of misery. We can look at this colossal sum of human tragedy without being gripped one whit. If we look into the soul of one woman these figures become invested with a new and terrible meaning.

Such an opportunity was strangely given me as we stood in a long queue outside the American embassy waiting for the passports that would make our personages sacrosanct when the German raiders took the city. A perspiring line, we shuffled slowly forward, thanking God that we were not as the Europeans, but had had the good sense to be born Americans. While in the next breath we tiraded against the self-same Government for not hurrying the American fleet to the rescue.

The alien-looking gentleman behind me mopped his brow and muttered something about wishing that he had not thirsted for other "joys than those of old St. Louis."

"Pennsylvania has her good points, too," I responded.

That random shot opened wide to me the gates of Romance and High Adventure. It broke the long silence of the girl just ahead.

"It's comforting just to hear the name of one's own home state," she said. "I lived in a little village in the western part of Pennsylvania," and, incidentally, she named the village where my father had once been minister of the church. I explained as much to her and marveled at the coincidence.

"More marvel still," she said, "for we come not only from the same state and the same village, but from the same house. My father was minister in that same church."

Nickleville is the prosaic name of that little hamlet in western Pennsylvania. Any gentle reader with a cynic strain there may verify this chronicle and find fresh confirmation for the ancient adage that "Fact is stranger far than Fiction."

That selfsame evening we held reunion in a café off the *Boulevard Clichy*. There I first discerned the slightness of her frame and marveled at the spirit that filled it. She was exuberant in the joy of meeting a countryman and, with the device of laughter, she kept in check the sadness which never quite came welling up in tears.

She was typical American but let her bear here the name by which her new friends in France called her - Marie. One might linger upon her large eyes and golden hair, but this is not the epic of a fair face but of a fair soul - vigorous and determined, too. To the power therein even the stolid waiter paid his homage.

"Pardon," he interjected once, "we must close now. The orders are for all lights out by nine. It is the government. They fear the Zeppelins."

"But that's just what I'm afraid of, too," Marie answered. "How can you turn us out into that darkness filled with Zeppelins?" He succumbed to this radiant banter and, covering every crevice that might emit a ray of light, he let us linger on long after closing time.

Marie's was one of those classic souls which by some anomaly, passing by the older lineages and cultures of the East, find birth-place in a bleak untutored village of the West. To this bareness some succumb, and the divine afflatus dies. Still others roam restlessly up and down, searching until they find their milieu and then for the first time their spirit glows.

Music had breathed upon this girl's spirit, touched with a vagabond desire. To satisfy it she must have money. So she gave lessons to children. Then a publisher bought some little melodies that she had set to words. And lastly, grave and reverend committeemen, after hesitating over her youth, made her head of music in a university of western Montana.

Early in 1914, with her gold reserves grown large enough for the venture, she set sail for the siege of Paris. To her charm and sterling worth it had soon capitulated - a quicker victory than she had dared to hope for. Around her studio in a street off the Champs Élysées she gathered a coterie of kindred souls. She told of the idealism and *camaraderie* of the little circle, while its foibles she touched upon with much merriment. Behind this outward jesting I gained a glimpse of the fight she had made for her advance.

"It's been hard," I said, "but what a lot you have found along the way."

"Yes, far more than you can imagine," she replied; "I have found Robert le Marchand."

"And who is he?"

"Well, he is an artist and an athlete, and he is just back from Albania - where he had most wonderful adventures. He has written them up for *'Gaulois.'* His home is in Normandy. And he is heir to a large estate in Italy in the South - in what looks like the heel on the map. And he has a degree from the Sorbonne and he is the real prince of our little court. And, best of all, he loves me."

Then she told the story of her becoming the princess of the little court.

"From his ancestral place in Italy," she said, "Robert sent me baskets of fruit gathered in his groves by his own hands. In one he placed a sprig of orange-blossoms. We laughed about it when we met again and ——"

I saw that after this affairs had ripened to a quick conclusion. In drives along the boulevards, in walks through the moonlit woods, at dinners, concerts, dances - these two mingled their dreams for their home in Normandy. The only discord in this summer symphony was a frowning father.

Marie was the epitome of all charms and graces. Yes. But she came undowered - that was all. And firm he stood against any breach in the long established code of his class. But they did not suffer this to disturb their plans and reveries, and through those soft July days they roamed together in their lotus-land. Then suddenly thundered that dream-shattering cannon out of the north.

"I was out of town for the week end," Marie continued; "I heard the beating of the 'General' and at call for mobilization I flew back here as quickly as I could. It was too late. There was only a note saying that he had gone, and how hard it was to go without one farewell."

"Now what are you going to do?"

"What can I do with Robert gone and all his friends in the army too?"

"Let me do what I can. Let me play substitute," I volunteered.

"Do you really mean what you just said?" she queried.

"I really do," I answered.

"Well, then, do you paddle a canoe?"

"Yes, but what has that to do with the question?" I replied perplexedly.

"Everything," she responded. "Robert is stationed at Corbeille, fifteen miles below here on the Seine. I have the canoe and to-morrow I want yon to go with me down the river to Robert."

My mind made a swift diagnosis of the situation. All exits from Paris carefully watched; suspicion rife everywhere - strangers off in a canoe; a sentinel challenge and a shot from the bank.

"Let us first consider ——" I began.

"We can do that in the canoe to-morrow," she interrupted.

And I capitulated, quite as Paris had.

We stepped out into the darkness that cloaked the silent city from its aerial ravagers. As we walked I mused upon this modern maiden's Iliad. While a thousand hug the quiet haven, what was it that impelled the one to cut moorings and range the deep? A chorus of croaking frogs greeted our turn into a park.

"Funny," said Marie, "but frogs drove me out of Nickleville! There was nothing to do at home but to listen to their eternal noise; to save my nerves I simply had to break away."

The prospect of that canoe trip was not conducive to easy slumber. The frog chorus in that Pennsylvania swamp, why had it not been less demonstrative? Still lots could happen before morning. One might develop appendicitis or the Germans might get the city. With these two comforting hopes I fell asleep. Morning realizing neither of them, I walked over to Marie's studio.

"Well, then, all ready for the expedition?" I said, masking my pessimism with a smile.

For reply she handed this note which read:

"Dear Marie: I have been transferred from Corbeille to Melun. It makes me ill to be getting ever farther and farther away. - Robert."

With the river trip cancelled, life looked more roseate to me. "And now we can't go after all," I said, mustering this time the appearance of sadness.

"Oh, don't look so relieved," she laughed, "because we're going anyhow."

"But what's the use? He has gone."

"Well, we are going where he has gone, that's all," she retorted.

I pointed out the facts that only military trains were running to

Melun; that we weren't soldiers; that the river was out of the question; that we had no aeroplane and that we couldn't go overland in a canoe.

"But we can with our wits," Marie added.

I explained how lame my wits were in French, and that two consecutive sentences would bring on trial for high treason to the language.

"Oh, but you don't furnish the wits," Marie retorted. "You just furnish the body."

In her plan of campaign I gathered that I was to act as a kind of convoy, from which she was to dart forth, torpedoing all obstacles. I was quite confident of her torpedoing ability but not of my fitness to play a star part as a dour and fear-inspiring background.

She packed her bag and presently we were making our way to the station through a blighted city.

At the Gare du Nord a cordon of soldiers had been thrown about the station; crowds surged up against the gates, a few frantically pleading and even crying to get through. The guards, to every plea and threat returned a harsh *"C'est impossible."* Undaunted by the despair of others, she looked straight into the eyes of the somber gate-keeper and, with every art, told the story of Robert le Marchand, brave young officer of France; of his American girl and his deep longing for her. When she had stirred this lethargic functionary into a show of interest in this girl, with a revealing gesture she said: "And here she is; please. Monsieur, let me go."

"Ah, Mademoiselle, I would like to," he replied, "but are not all the soldiers of France longing for wives and sweethearts? *Mon Dieu!* if they all rode there would be no room for the *militaire.* The Boches would take us in the midst of our farewells. There is never any end to leave-takings."

"But, Monsieur, I did not have one good-by."

"No, Mademoiselle. *C'est impossible.*"

The guardian of the second gate took her plea in a way that did more credit to his heart than to his knowledge of geography. He thought (and we made no effort to disillusionize him) that she had come all the way from America since the outbreak of war. It nearly moved him to tears.

Was he surrendering? Almost. But recovering his official negative head-shake and trusting not to words, he fell back upon the formula: "No, Madame, *c'est impossible.*"

The truth had failed and so had the half-truth. To the next forbidding guard Marie came as a Red Cross nurse, hurrying to her station.

"Your uniform, Madame," he interposed.

"No time to get a uniform; no time to get a permission," she explained.

"Take time, Madame," was his brusque dismissal.

Each time rebuffed, she tried again, but against the full battery of her blandishments the line was adamant.

"It's no use," I said. "We may as well go home."

"No retreat until we've tried our last reserves," she responded, clinking some coins together in her hand. "We'll try a change of tactics."

We reconnoitered and decided that an opening might be made through guardian number two. He had almost surrendered in the first engagement. This time, along with the smile, she flashed a coin. Perchance he had already repented of his first refusal. Anyhow, if an officer of France could be made happy with his sweetheart and at the same time a brave gendarme could be made richer by a five-franc piece, would not La Belle France fight so much the better? The logic was incontestable. "This way, Mademoiselle, Monsieur, and be quick, please."

We had passed through the lines into a riot of red and blue uniforms. Soldiers were everywhere sprawled over the platforms, knotted up in sleep, yawning, stretching their limbs, eating, smoking and swearing. No one knew anything about tickets, trains or aught else.

Swirled about in an eddying tide of entraining troops, we were flung up against a stationary being garbed as a railway dispatcher. He bluffed and blustered a bit. Our story, however, supplemented by some hard cash, procured calm and presently we found ourselves in a compartment with two tickets marked Melun, a few rations and sundry admonitions not to converse with fellow-passengers until the train started.

It is hard to explain why any one should want to communicate in German to an American girl in a French railway compartment in wartime. But explain why some people want to play with trip-hammers and loaded guns. We know they do. And so, though aware that there were spy-hunting listeners all around, a mad desire to utter the forbidden tongue obsessed me. Wry faces from Marie, emphasized by repeated pinches at each threatened outbreak, brought me back to my senses and to Anglo-Saxon.

Not only one who spoke, but even one who understood the hated tongue was a suspect. For the least knowledge of the enemy's language was to some the hall-mark of a spy. The game played throughout France and Belgium was to fling a sudden command at the suspect, catching the unwary fellow off-guard, and thus trap him into self-betrayal.

An official would say sharply: *"Nehmen Sie ihre Hutte ab"* (Take off your hat). Or there would come a sudden challenge on the street, *"Wohin gehen Sie?"* (Where are you going?) If instinctively one obeyed or replied in German, he was there caught with the goods.

Our major domo under the influence of the coin, or what he had procured at the vintner's in exchange therefor, grew a bit playful. He suddenly flung open the door and cried, *"Steigen Sie auf."* If I had comprehended his meaning involuntarily I would have obeyed, but luckily my brain has a slow shifting language gear. By the time it began dawning upon me that we had been told to vacate the car Marie had fixed me with her eyes and gripped me like a vise with her hand so that I knew that I was to stay put. One man involuntarily started and then checked himself. He was so patently a Frenchman though that everybody laughed. The major domo chuckled and marched away, much pleased with his playful humor.

At last, with much jolting, we started on our crawling journey. Sometimes the snail-pace would be accelerated; our hopes would then expand, only to collapse again with a bang. Again we would be sidetracked to let coal-cars, cattle cars and flat cars with guns go by. Civilians were ciphers in the new order, and if it served any military purpose to dump us into the river, in we would have gone with no questions asked. We sat about, a wilted and dispirited lot. Occasionally some one would thrust his head out the window to observe progress. He

127

was generally rewarded by a view of the Eiffel Tower from a new angle, for it seemed that we were simply being shunted in and about and all around the city.

The most icy reserve must find itself cracked and thawing in the intimacies which a jerking railway car precipitates. There is no dignity which is proof against a sound bump upon the head. Thus our irritations and suspicions gave way to laughter, and laughter brings all the barriers down. The compartment became a confessional. The anxious looking man opposite was hoping to get to his estate and to bury a few of his most treasured things before the Germans came. The two young fellows with scraggly beards were brothers, given five days' leave to see a dying father; three days had been spent in a vain effort to get started there. Another man had a half telegram which read, "Accident at home you ——" Not another word had he been able to get through. The silent young man in the corner smiled pleasantly when his turn came but volunteered no information. I likewise passed.

Marie, wishing to fortify herself with all possible help in her venture, told her tale in full. An immediate proffer came from the hitherto taciturn young man in the corner. "Why, this is romance in earnest. I do wish that I might be of some help," he said with genuine interest.

Our new friend we found had for a grandfather no less a dignitary than Alexander Dumas. His name he told us was Louis Dumas, an artist, not yet called to the colors, and bound now for Villeneuve, "and before we can really get acquainted, here we are," he said as the train came to a stop.

As he stepped to the door it was flung open by an officer who shouted, "Everybody out! This car is for the military." We protested. We displayed our tickets. The officer laughed and, seizing one reluctant passenger, dragged him out. A quickly ejected and much dejected band, we found ourselves upon the street of a little outlying village nine miles from Paris. It had taken half as many hours to get there.

We fell upon the one village gendarme with a volley of questions. By pitching her voice above the hubbub, Marie got in her inquiry about the distance to Melun.

"Thirty kilometers by the main road," he answered.

This, then, was the issue of that tense day of strategy and daring: to be stranded in this suburb from which it was impossible to go forward to Melun and almost as difficult to return to Paris. Marie crumpled under the blow and then I realized how much it had cost her to maintain that calm outward demeanor.

By sheer will-power she had kept the tears from her eyes and the tremor from her limbs. Long held in leash, they now leaped out to possess her.

Dumas ran hither and thither, hunting conveyance but in vain. Three of his friends had automobiles. He called them by telephone. All cars had been commandeered. He stood with head drooping in real dejection.

"Ah, I have it!" he exclaimed, "my friend Veilleau, he has an aeroplane and he will do it."

This was quite too much even for Marie's soaring spirit; but she scarcely had time to picture herself ranging the sky when Dumas was back again, sorrowfully confessing failure. Aeroplanes likewise had heard the tocsin; they had sterner business than wafting lovers through the sky; they were carrying explosives and messages in the service of France. Dumas looked almost as disappointed as the wilted little figure he was trying to help.

When the villagers understood her plight, they were full of sympathy, full of condolences, but also full of tales of arrest for those traveling on the main road.

"Where was this road, anyhow?"

"Out there," they replied.

Turning a corner, we looked down the long row of poplars that lined the main road to Melun.

CHAPTER XIII
AMERICA IN THE ARMS OF FRANCE

ANY POPLAR-FRINGED road in France holds its strange lure. Dignity and grace lie in these tall swaying trees sentinelling the way on either side. To the poet, it is at all times the way to Arcady. But at eventide when the mystic light comes streaming from the west, touching the billowing green into gold, then even to the prosaic there is a call from the whispering, wind-stirred leaves to go a-grailing and to find at the end the palace or the princess. This time it was the prince who was calling. This little sad-featured girl was a-tune to hear his call. Perhaps in the purple mist she could even see her prince and feel the pleading of those outstretched arms. Wistfully she looked down her road to Arcady; but how far away the end and so bestrewn with terrors.

Are psychic forces subject to ordinary physical laws, and do they act most powerfully along unobstructed ways? At any rate the voltage was high in the psychic currents that swept the straight road to Melun that afternoon, for when this saddened girl turned from her long gaze down the road to Melun it was with a transfigured face. Her tear-dimmed eyes shone with a calm resolve and the uplifted chin foreboded, I perceived, no good to my dreams of rest and resignation.

To know the worst I ventured: "Well, how are we going to get to Paris?"

"You mean Melun?" she gently smiled.

"Sheer madness," I replied. "A carriage is out of the question, and if we had one there would be a hundred guards to turn us back."

We stepped aside while two military trucks in their gray war-paint went lurching by. She followed them with her eyes until they disappeared into the distant haze where poplar and purple sky melted into one.

"Going straight to Robert," she cried, clasping her hands, "and if they only knew how much I want to go, I don't believe they would refuse me."

Preposterous as it was, if they could indeed have seen the longing in her eyes I felt certain they wouldn't either. Discreetly I refrained from saying so.

We walked slowly back to the partial barricade which compelled the motors to slow down. A siren heralded the approach of a car. I drew her aside into the ditch. Wrenching her hand loose she cried:

"I don't care what happens. I'm going to stop this car!" Planting herself squarely in the path of the great gray thing, she signaled wildly for it to stop. The goggled driver bore straight down upon the little figure, then swerving sharply to one side jammed on the brakes and came to a sudden halt.

"What's the trouble?" said the other occupant of the car, a thick-set swarthy fellow in a captain's uniform. "Washout, bombs or Uhlans?"

"No, it's Robert!" Marie exclaimed.

"Robert?" he cried, angered at this delay. His aroused curiosity took the sting out of his words as he exclaimed, "Who the devil is Robert?"

She told him who Robert was, told it with her soul flaming in her face. Her voice implored. Her eyes entreated. The black cloud that had overcast the captain's countenance at the impertinence of her action melted slowly away into a genial smile. And yet had fortune been unkind she might have brought us some calculating routinist with pride in strict obedience to the letter of the military law.

"It's a plain infraction of all the regulations," he said, "but if you can risk all this for him, I can risk this much for you. Step up," he added, lifting her into a seat, and giving me a place behind with the baggage. It had happened all too swiftly for comprehension. We were on the road to Arcady again - and this time in high estate. With fifty horses racing away under the hood of our royal car, we were speeding forward like a bullet.

Adown this road in the days of chivalry traveled oft the noble chevaliers and knights. In shining cavalcades they rode forth for glory in their lady's name. But never was there truer tribute to the spirit of High

Romance than when down this same road, athrone upon a war-gray car, came this little Pennsylvania music-teacher.

All the way we rode exalted, with hearts too full for speech. And our benefactor gave us no occasion for it. His eyes were fixed straight ahead upon the speeding road, alert for obstacles or rapt in visions of his own dear ones; or, more probable still, deep in reconsideration of his rashness in harboring two strangers who might turn out to be traitors.

"Ten spies were shot here in the last two days," was his one laconic communication. As the Romanesqne towers of Melun's Notre Dame came into view, he drew up by a post which marked a mile from the city, saying,

"The rest of the way I believe you had better go on foot." With a polite bow and a smile he bade us adieu and was off, leaving us quite non-plussed. But the swift ride had driven refreshment and resolution into us. After some spirited passages with a few astounded sentries, we found ourselves in the city of our quest.

It was a small garrison center. Into it now from every side had poured rivulets of soldiers until the street shimmered with its red and blue. Melun had changed rôles with Paris. A desert quiet brooded over the gay capital, while this drab provincial place was now athrum with activity - not the activity of parade but of the workshop. The air was vibrant with the clangor of industry. Everywhere soldiers were cleaning guns, grooming horses, piling sacks. The only touch to lighten this depressing dead-in-earnestness came from a group of soldiers engaged in filling a huge bolster. They playfully tried to push one of their number in with the straw. In one doorway two men were seeking to render their uniforms less of a target by inking their brass-buttons black, while two rollicking fellows perched high upon a bread-wagon were making the welkin ring with vociferous demands for passage way. That was what everybody wanted.

We, too, pressed forward into the throng. Enough other civilians were scattered amidst the masses of soldiery to render us not too conspicuous. And such a weltering anarchy it was: men, horses, and guns jammed together in one grand promiscuous jumble. Who was to organize discipline and victory out of such a turmoil? But that there was a directing mind moving through this democratic chaos, the Germans later learned to know full well. Likewise, the two strangers congratulating themselves on being lost in the vast confusion.

To get our bearings we seated ourselves in a small café, and were intently poring over a map when a shuffling noise made us look up. A detachment of soldiers was entering the café. Much to our astonishment, they came to attention in front of us. They constituted the spy-hunting squad. All day they walked the city on the trail of suspects. To trap a prospective victim, and just as they were relishing the shooting of him to be compelled to release him, and then to drag on to the next prospect, and to repeat the process was not inspiriting. Apparently luck had gone against them, but at sight of us a new hope lit their eyes.

Two officers, bowing politely, said: "Pardon, Monsieur; pardon, Madame! Your papers."

Being held up as a spy, however nerve-racking, contributes considerably to one's sense of self-importance. It's a rare thrill for a civilian to be waited on by a reception committee in full dress uniform.

But this was by all odds the most imposing array of military yet. I remember being distinctly impressed by the comic opera setting; the gay costumed soldiers in a crowded French café, the big American and the little heroine. In a moment the soldier chorus would go rollicking off singing some ditty like:

"Let high respect come to their station,
For they are members of a mighty nation."

I deliberated for a few seconds, for presently our papers like talismen would exorcise all dangers. With a gesture suitably sweeping for the dose of this act, I smiled assuringly, reached into that inner right-hand pocket, and felt a terrific thump of the heart as I clutched an empty void and forthwith drew out an empty hand. The smile turned a little sickly. I repeated. Likewise a third time. The smile died and a cold sweat gathered on my brow. It was now more like a Turkish bath than a comic opera. The rollicking soldier chorus began to look curiously like a band of assassins.

I was positive that I had tucked these papers in that pocket. Had some evil spirit whisked them away? I conducted a frantic and furious search through every pocket. As one after an- other they turned out empty an increasing gloom settled down upon my face, and upon the faces of the assassins was registered a corresponding increment of joy.

Reader, have you ever been warden of the theater tickets? As your party thronged up to the entrance, do you remember the stand-still of your heart when you found that the tickets weren't in the pocket that you put them, followed by the discovery that they weren't in any other pocket? Do you remember spasmodically ramming your hands into all your pockets until your arms took on the motions of a sailor at the pump, trying to save the old ship at sea? Remember the black looks insinuating you were an idiot and the growing conviction on your part that they were not far wrong? Multiply and intensify all these sensations a thousandfold and you will get a faint idea of how one feels when he is trying to locate his passports and the officials are hoping that he can't.

Several months elapsed in as many seconds. To break the appalling silence, I began gibbering away in a jargon compound of gesticulation, English and remnants of High School French. Why, oh, why wouldn't somebody say something? At last the *commissionaire*, hitherto impassive, said:

"Vielleicht Sie konnen Deutsch sprechen."

("Perhaps you can speak German.")

It was so kind of him that I plunged head-long into the net.

"Ja ich kann Deutsch sprechen," I fairly shouted.

("Yes, I can speak German.")

I would have confessed to Chinese or Russian, so anxious was I to get on speaking terms with some one.

"So you speak German," said the *commissionaire* significantly; "I thought as much." The soldiers looked at their Lebel rifles as though the not unpleasant duty of making them speak for France would soon be theirs. In their eyes now I was a German spy and Marie was my accomplice. I began to be almost convinced of it myself.

Now if this were fiction and not just a straight setting down of facts the papers might here be produced by a breathless courier or dropped from an aeroplane. But they weren't.

At this crisis when all seemed lost, Marie rallied. She said: "Look in the lining of your coat."

I was unaware of any hole in the lining but, duly obedient, I reached inside and found an opening. Some papers rustled in my hand. I clutched them like a madman, violently drew them forth and, perceiving that they were the precious documents, waved them about like a dancing dervish. The soldiers were distinctly disappointed and cast an evil eye on Marie, as though holding her personally responsible for cheating them out of a little target-practice.

The *commissionaires* examined the papers, smiled as graciously as before they had frowned and, with the crestfallen soldiers resuming their old look of boredom, they disappeared as mysteriously as they had come.

Out into the gathering gloom we followed too, and trudged to the barracks upon the hill.

At the entrance the familiar "Quiva là?" (Who goes there?) rang a challenge to our approach. We informed the subaltern that it was Sergeant le Marchand that we sought.

A confusion of calls echoed through the court. An orderly then announced that Robert le Marchand was sick; this was followed by the report that he was out; then some more conflicting reports, followed by Robert le Marchand himself. A new-lit lantern in the archway diffused a wan light around his pale face while he peered forward into the dusk. He could not see at first, but as by a dream-voice out of the mist came his name, twice repeated: "Robert, Robert."

Was this some torturing hallucination? Before he had time to consider that, the reality flung herself into his arms. Again and again he clasped the nestling figure, as if to assure himself that it was not an apparition that he held but his very own sweetheart.

They stood there in the archway, quite oblivious to the passing soldiers. The soldiers seemed to understand and, smiling approval of this new entente - America in the arms of France - they silently passed along.

The first transports of surprise and joy being over, he begged for an explanation of this miracle. Briefly I sketched the doings of the day, and as he saw this wisp of a girl braving all dangers for love's sake, he was in one moment terror-stricken at the risks she had run, and in the next aglow with admiration for her splendid daring. Dangers had haloed her and he sat silent like a worshiper.

"Instead of a tragedy," he exclaimed, "it's like a story with a happy ending. But let me tell how narrowly we escaped a tragic ending," he added, drawing Marie closer to him.

On the fifth of August it seems that his squad had been stationed upon the bridge over the Seine at Corbeille. The orders were to prevent any passage over the bridge and under the bridge - particularly the latter, as the authorities suspected an attempt upon the part of enemy plotters to use the waterways in and out of Paris. Traffic had been suspended and orders had been explicit: "Shoot any watercraft, without challenge, as it turns the bend at the Corbeille bridge."

Corbeille had been the objective of our proposed canoe journey. There had been abundant warrant then in the very constitution of things for my psychic shivers at the first broaching of that canoe-trip.

Our escape had been by a narrow margin. If that telegram, "Left Corbeille and gone to Melun," had missed us, Robert le Marchand's first shot might have meant death, not to his enemy but to his own life and soul. On the eve of the great war he might have embraced his dearest one cold and lifeless. But instead of that somber ending, here she was, warm, radiant and laughing - doubly precious by the trials through which she had passed and the death from which she had been delivered.

CHAPTER XIV
NO-MAN'S-LAND

THE MOVEMENTS OF the *231ier Regiment d'Infanterie* were publicly announced. It was scheduled to entrain on the morrow for the front between Metz and Nancy. Robert le Marchand needed not to go. Pronounced unfit by the regimental doctor, his name had been placed upon the hospital list. Amidst the bustle of preparation for departure he spent the day in quietude, and Marie played nurse to the invalid.

Her little tale about being a Red Cross worker told at the Gare du Nord turned out to be the truth and not the fable that she had fancied. Robert's recovery was so rapid that the doctor was astonished. He was understanding, however; also he was a very kindly doctor. He came and smiled and nodded his approval. Then he went away, still leaving Robert on the sick list.

A long season of such delightful convalescence was now his for the taking. Golden days they promised to be to him and to Marie, but to France those early August days held portents of defeat and disaster. So one gathered from the ugly rumors from the frontier. The great battle raging in the north had its miniature in their souls. Theirs to choose days of ease and dalliance or the call to duty.

When the 231st regiment formed into line the afternoon of August 7th, the sergeant, radiant and happy, was with them again. But the tears in his eyes? That perplexed his comrades. Those who knew the secret let the romance lose none of its glamour in the telling until Marie became, forsooth, the heroine of the regiment.

At four o'clock the regimental band struck up the *Marseillaise* and the regiment moved down the road. The sergeant's feet kept time with his marching men, while his eyes turned to the blue figure on a balcony, whose hand was fluttering a limp white handkerchief. She was striving her best to wave a cheerful farewell.

The repeated strains: "Ye sons of France awake to glory," came each time more faintly as the regiment moved steadily away. There is always pain in such a growing distance. But it was not all pain to the tear-stained girl upon the balcony. She had her part in that glory. Had she not, too, made her sacrifice.

It was quite as if the regiment had sailed away under sealed orders. Metz and Nancy had been broadcasted about as the objective of the 231st. But that had been just a blind for German informers. For the next *communiqué* mentioning the regiment came from far to the west, where it had been hurried to hold up the grave threat upon Paris. At Soissons the gray-green advance rolled itself up against the red and blue of the 231st.

Back and forth the battle line surged through the old streets, now lurid with the light of blazing houses. A shell falling on the town-hall fired this ancient land-mark. A great flame-fountain burst up from the heart of the city. "Rescue the archives!" was the cry. For this, volunteers were called. The dash of a sergeant and his men into the burning hall and back again through the bullet-spattered streets is related in the *Journal Officiel*. It tells of the safe return of the archives, but of few survivors. For impetuous valor in this exploit, the name of Sergeant le Marchand was changed to Lieutenant le Marchand.

That was my last tidings of Marie and Robert, until a year later a letter came to me in a shaky but familiar hand. It had the post-mark of Hornell Sanitarium, New York. It was from Marie, and one glance revealed the tragedy. Briefly it was this:

In the attempted Champagne drive of 1915 the 231st regiment was ordered to rush the barbed wire barricade and drive a wedge into the enemy's line. At command Lieutenant le Marchand leaped from cover to lead the charge of his men. Scarcely had he uttered his cry, "En avant!" when he was dropped in his tracks, a bullet through his brain. Over his body, with revenge adding to their fury, the regiment swept like mad. The trenches, a quarry of prisoners, and the thrill of high praise from the general were theirs - a triumph with a bitter taste, for some, creeping back, had found their young lieutenant crumpled where he fell, the moonlight cold upon his blood-stained face. "In order that France might live he was willing to close his eyes upon her forever." Curiously his sword was sticking upright just as it had dropped from his hand. They buried him where he lay upon the edge of No-Man's-Land. Tears were showered on his grave, and on that fatal bullet many bitter curses.

But this does not complete the tale of murder wrought by that slug of lead. Each plunging bullet blazes its black trail of the spirit-killed.

A month later and three thousand miles away this German missile struck the heart of an American girl with a more cruel impact than it had struck the brain of this lieutenant of France. She, too, crumpled and fell upon the thorns. His had been a speedy, painless death; one sharp electric stroke and then the closing night. A like oblivion would have been sweet to her. But she had to face it out alone. Upon her torn heart were beaten a thousand hammer-strokes, and through the endless nights she bore the anguish of a thousand deaths.

The death-lists of Europe hold 5,000,000 other names besides Lieutenant le Marchand's. Behind each name there marches with springless steps one or more figures shrouded in black.

A year later one of these figures arose from her burial alive, a whitened shadow of her former self.

"I know that I ought not to have collapsed, just as I know that I ought not to hate the Germans," Marie wrote. "I'm pulling myself together now, and I am trying to work and to forgive. But my thoughts are always wandering out to just one spot - that is where Robert lies. When peace comes I'm going straight over there and with my own hands I shall dig through every trench until I find him."

Tragic futility indeed! One recompense for the colossal slaughter and the long war; few shall ever find their dead.

On a recent Sunday morning I stepped into a church of a Lake City of the West. The organ was filling the large structure with its sounds; gradually out of the dim light came the face of the player.

A hard road had she traveled since last I saw her, a trim little blue-clad figure waving good-by from that balcony in Melun. It was not strange that her face was white. There was nothing strange either in the passion of that music.

These experiences of Gethsemane and Calvary had been first enacted in her own soul. The organ was but giving voice to them. There was a plaintive touch in the minor chords, as if pleading for days that were gone. It climbed to a closing rapture, as if two who had parted here had, for the moment, hailed each other in the world of Souls.

AFTERWORD

I T SEEMS SOMETIMES as if the torch of civilization had been almost extinguished in this deluge of blood. This darkening of the face of the earth has cost more than the blood and treasure of the race - it has involved a terrific strain on the mind and soul of man.

The blasting of hundreds of villages, the sinking of thousands of ships, and the killing of millions of men is no small monument to the power of the human will. Deplore as we may the sanguinary ends to which this will has been bent, it has at any rate shown itself to be no weakling. We must marvel at the grim tenacity with which it has held to its goal through the long red years.

But now it is challenged by an infinitely bigger task.

The great nations sundered apart by this hideous anarchy have become hissings and bywords to each other. One group has been cast outside the Pale to become the Ishmaels of the universe. The purpose is to keep them there.

Yet try as we may we cannot live upon a totally disrupted planet without bringing a common disaster upon us all. It may be a matter of decades and generations but eventually the reconciliation must come.

To start civilization on the upward path again, to make the world into a neighborhood anew, to achieve the moral unity of humanity, is that infinitely bigger task with which the human will is challenged. As in the last years it has relentlessly concentrated its energies upon the Great War, now through the next decades and generations it must as steadfastly hold them to the Great Reconciliation. The tragedy of it all is that humanity must go at this crippled by a hatred like add eating into the soul.

Villages will arise again from their ruins, the plow shall turn anew the shell-pitted fields into green meadow-lands, a kindly nature will soon obliterate the scars upon the landscape but not the deep searings on the soul. Europe must grapple with this work of reconstruction handicapped by this black devil poisoning the mind and vitiating every effort. The worst curse bequeathed to the coming generations is not the mountain of debt but this heritage of hate.

It does not behoove Americans to stand on inviolate shores and prate of the wickedness of wrath. Moreover, this evil is not to be exorcised by a pious wish for it not to be. It is. And there is every excuse under the arch of heaven for its existence.

If we had felt the eagles' claws tearing at our flesh; if, like Europe, our soil was crimsoned with the blood of our murdered; if millions of our women were breaking their hearts in anguish - we too would consider it a gratuitous bit of impertinence to be told not to cherish rancor towards those who had unleashed the hell-hounds of lust and carnage upon us.

As it is, we are not sacrosanct. Three thousand miles have not sufficed to keep the deadly virus out of our system. The violation of Belgium kindled a fire against the invaders which the successive cruelties served to fan into a flaming resentment.

Then came our own losses - a mere grazing of the skin alongside of the bleeding white of Europe. But it has touched us deep enough to rouse even a sense of vindictiveness. This kept to ourselves will do injury to ourselves alone. But when we shout or whisper across the seas that we too despise the barbarians we help no one. We simply help to render the heart-breaking task of reconciliation well-nigh impossible by lashing to a wilder fury the people already blinded, embittered and frenzied by their own hate. Those who, above the luxury of giving full rein to their own passions, put the welfare of the French, English, Belgians and other broken peoples of earth, will do everything in their power to eradicate this gangrene from their souls.